B*Go For* roker

An executive's guide to hiring a broker
for today's complex real estate deals

John J. Culbertson

CCIM, CRE, SIOR

Brian,

its a fellow SIOR,
I hope you enjoy the
book!

Respectfully

John

704-XXX-XXX

ISBN: 0615897673
ISBN 13: 9780615897677

Praise for Go For Broker

John Culbertson's book is absolutely entertaining - the story of his quest for a "better way to broker" and decision to found his own firm is valuable as a case study in entrepreneurship - and the book is packed with insight into how C-suite executives at mid-sized companies can take a more rational approach to meeting their real estate needs. Just as important, John's got a unique personal story to tell and a powerful underlying message to communicate about how a passionate commitment to process gives professionals the freedom to think and problem-solve creatively, benefiting them and their clients. Highly recommended.

Tim Whitmire, DealCloud, Inc.

"The whole world of commercial real estate becomes increasingly complex and complicated every year, and many executives who are confident experts in their own fields and professions lose confidence in dealing with one of the most important investments and expenditures. John Culbertson has created a powerful, comprehensive but simple process for executives to think through their real estate future in a strategic and systematic fashion. Everything in this book has been successfully tested in the marketplace. Being a business owner myself with extensive and expanding commercial requirements, I appreciate enormously the practical wisdom and simple framework that John provides to serious and committed readers."

- Dan Sullivan, Founder, The Strategic Coach Inc.

"For most companies, real estate is ubiquitous and indispensable. And because it affects everyone in the organization, it is not easy to manage. **Go For Broker is a game plan for executives to succinctly communicate their objectives to a real estate service provider.** There have been numerous times where I have encountered the principal-agent conflict discussed in this book, and I was fortunate to have great people around me who were, as the book describes, "selfless agent advocates". Without them, the transactions would have gotten complex, resulting in procrastination and missed deadlines. **I recommend Go For Broker for anyone interested in hiring a real estate brokerage team who has a clear focus on the client's needs over their own."**

- John B. McCoy, Director, AT&T and
Former Chairman, BankOne Corporation

"In our practice, we work with many of the top producers in the commercial real estate brokerage industry. Like John, they all drive an incredible amount of value to their clients thanks to their discipline, passion and proper perspective. **The methods and processes that John uses are some of the best in the industry. Any executive reading this book will enjoy the read and gather many tips on how to effectively navigate both common and complex real estate transactions".**

- Rod Santomassimo, Author "Brokers Who Dominate" and
Founder, The Massimo Group

"Real estate is crucial to almost every organization, yet the process by which it is bought, sold and leased is poorly understood. Even full-time professionals often spend years in the business before truly understanding the key dynamics. *Go for Broker* **cuts through the fog, and explains how real estate deals actually get done**. Even more importantly, it will help to ensure that the process works for you. **It should be read at least once by anyone who might be buying, selling or leasing commercial real estate."**

- Lee Roberts, Chief Operating Officer, VantageSouth Bank

"This book should be read by all real estate professionals and all laymen who have occasion to interact with the real estate transaction process. The necessary involvement of intermediaries is generally the point at which the experience of buying, selling or leasing property becomes a trap for the unwary, frequently resulting in disappointment and disillusionment. As John's compact and instructive book emphasizes, this need not be the inevitable result. **Readable, thoughtful and cogent, I would particularly recommend its reading to all users of these brokerage services.**

I know from firsthand experience, John practices what he preaches. His belief that a process of continuing quality improvement, open and early communication of goals and objectives and measuring attainment of results as a basis for incentive compensation, are practices that the real estate industry as a whole would be well served to incorporate as standard procedure."

- Phillip Norwood - Former CEO, Faison Capital Advisors and
Vice chairman, Trammell Crow Company

"John possesses a unique set of qualities that distinguish him from many other brokers, real estate consultants and analysts. **His skill set is equal parts intellectual, relational and street savvy.** He adds a higher level of analysis and processes to his core strengths which are market knowledge, relationships and decades of experience."

- Mason Zimmerman, Senior Vice President - Pope and Land Enterprises, Inc.

"**This is a great book for anyone hiring a broker to be a true advocate in a deal. There are simple tips to ensure you hire the right broker - which is one who you can delegate to; one who provides order to complex negotiations; and gives you confidence so that you can direct your attention to other tasks.** Culbertson's first special report on the brokerage game was being passed around by mutual clients. I received a copy and immediately shared it with our brokerage and development teams. We were introduced to Culbertson and brought him on board immediately"

- Scott MacLaren
President, North Carolina Operations, Stiles Corporation

"There is no question that the Great Recession increased the complexity of commercial real estate transactions. **It is refreshing and very helpful to have a resource like Go For Broker that demonstrates techniques to align interests, avoid conflicts of interest and help achieve our goals. John Culbertson makes Go For Broker enjoyable and I strongly recommend it to anyone hiring a real estate broker. I** have seen Cardinal Partners put these practices to work on challenging transactions and their process and integrity are models of excellence."

- Chris Bennett, CEO of 27eighteen

NOTE TO READER

No attorney believes anything a broker says, so reading this section was probably a waste of time.

Introduction

I was in high school and my Mom was studying for her master's degree in therapy when my family took a weeklong vacation in Georgia. We lived in Charlotte and drove down Interstate 85 and did all the things you usually did in Georgia in those days – visited the Coke museum, saw a Braves game, went to Stone Mountain, spent a day at Six Flags Over Georgia.

Except that on the sixth day, when other families would have headed back to North Carolina, my Mom took me – her youngest of four children, and the only one still living at home - on a side trip, to a testing center for the Johnson O'Connor Research Foundation, for a day and a half of aptitude testing.

Mom was diving deep into the world of therapy and counseling, and I was her guinea pig. It probably helped that I had developed a knack for changing schools yearly, frustrating teachers and educational administrators alike as I blazed a trail of infamy through the public and private schools of Mecklenburg County. If she kept testing me long enough, Mom probably figured, sooner or later she might get an answer that would solve all of her and my Dad's frustrations with me.

After all the testing, the Johnson O'Connor people sat us down in a room with a stack of dot matrix computer printouts and delivered their finding: I needed to spend more time working on my vocabulary. Johnson O'Connor decided a long time ago that success was directly related to a person's range of vocabulary and that everyone would benefit by a degree of knowledge that would be obtained by studying their books, which my well-intended mother was quick to buy.

That being said, they added, for another $500 and one more battery of tests, they would be able to pinpoint my ideal vocation in life.

Mom was game, so we stayed another day and I went through another round of tests.

This was it, the moment of truth, when my destiny would be revealed in bold, block letters composed of dozens of printed dot-matrix characters:

"B U S D R I V E R"

Luckily for Mom (and maybe me, as well), there were plenty of other aptitude assessments out there. Most of them, she assured me, were much more sophisticated tools than those Johnson O'Connor tests. The Kolbe System (3,3,8,7), The McQuaig Institute (Big D), The Strong Interest Inventory, The Institute for Personality and Ability, aptest, Astrologists (Libra), Cosmologists, Carlson Institute, COPS, TTI, Target Teams, The Center for Applied Cognitive Research, The Hollowell Center, DiSC, and, of course, the Myers Briggs (ENTJ).

And because she was curious and I wanted her to be happy we took them.

The results: Litigator. Photographer. Broadcaster. Marketing Executive. Florist. Banker. Lead singer for the Ramones.

Real estate developer.

Finally, here was something interesting. It was the 1980s. Fred Trammell Crow had turned his Dallas-based Trammell Crow Company into the country's first nationwide developer of commercial real estate. Skyscrapers built on spec by his company were the emblems of prosperity that populated the skylines of booming New South cities like Dallas, Atlanta and my hometown. Trammell Crow was one of the nation's top landlords, with interests at one time in an estimated 300 million square feet of developed real estate, the company behind the Peachtree Center in Atlanta, the Dallas Market Center and San Francisco's Embarcadero project.

Years before Donald Trump became the late-1980s poster boy for real estate flash (and trash) I studied Trammell Crow, clipping articles about him and his company, noting that the guys coming out of top MBA programs all seemed to be going into real estate development. They would go to work for a Trammell Crow or Childress Klein or one of the other big developers, who would give them a region or territory to oversee and they were off and running. With Trammell Crow leading the way, these mega-developers had created a template for the development of commercial real estate and scaled their operations to the national market. They'd turned the skyscraper – the ultimate emblem of reaching for the stars, the vessel for so many big dreams and shattered hopes over the decades – into a commodity.

I made my way into that world, first by way of a lucky connection, into a right-place, right-time company that was building warehouses (the same buildings that had given Trammell Crow his start in Dallas in the 1950s) next to airports, poised to take advantage of the just-in-time sea change in logistics and the supply chain that swept through the business world in the 1990s. I was a regional lead for the firm, overseeing pre-development due diligence and marketing, as we developed class-A distribution and office projects for likes of FedEx and others at BOS, JFK, CLT, DTW, SEA and LAX. Eventually the company, International Airport Centers, was sold to the largest industrial REIT in the United States.

Next, I fulfilled my childhood dream by going to work for Trammell Crow itself, where I got an inside view of what commercial real estate had become in the 21st century - a cozy insider's game where landlords and brokers golfed at Kiawah and skied at Vail. Tenants fell into three categories: those big enough and with the corporate will to get their way with brokers and landlords; those big enough not to care about real estate inefficiencies that amounted to nothing more than a rounding error on the balance sheet; and those left at the mercy of the landlord-broker alliance.

In 2006, I started my own commercial real estate brokerage, Cardinal Real Estate Partners (we became a partnership-of-one after the guy who was going to put the 's' at the end of our name got cold feet about leaving Trammell Crow at the last minute and ended up inheriting my job).

My intent: create a leading boutique real estate firm by focusing intently on clients, making my fees contingent on performance and putting a well-run process at the center of my service offering.

In the years since, I've sold everything from an empty pro basketball arena in Charlotte to tracts of timberland in South Carolina and a Tennessee coal mine to land speculators. I helped major landlords find graceful way out of binds when tenants decided to shutter their North Carolina offices during the real estate collapse. And I've assisted any number of small- to mid-sized businesses in figuring out their next steps.

In 20 years in the real estate "game" (make no mistake, this is a game - one that you should be playing to win) I've come to realize that the unique set of skills and insights I inherited from my parents made me into a unique creature in this business: a "real estate psychologist."

I've already told you about my mom, who gave me a curiosity about what makes people tick, and discovering their strengths and unique talents. My dad has spent decades as a successful estate planner and wealth manager. From him, I inherited the stubborn determination that got me through 18 bumpy years of primary, undergrad and graduate school, and I learned the touchstones of client service that have stayed with me to this day:

- Only give "pure" advice
- Ask good questions and take great notes
- Know your client's objectives
- Make the process clear and constructive
- Don't be a solo artist - surround yourself with smart people

Drawing on those lessons and my own experience in my first 20 years in commercial real estate, I built Cardinal to be a different kind of brokerage, based on what I think of as "a better way to broker."

I'm also just arrogant enough to think that the lessons I've learned from and about commercial real estate have widespread application, so I'll try to point out the places where I think there is a bigger lesson to be learned about how we do business in America in the 2010s.

I've set up the book so that each chapter hits a different major point, using key anecdotes to illustrate the following points:

- **Chapter 1: A Better Way to Broker**: How the commercial real estate brokerage model is broken and why extreme client advocacy is the solution.

- **Chapter 2: From Broker to Agent-Advocate:** How you can transform your relationship with your commercial broker, turning the broker into a truly useful agent-advocate.
- **Chapter 3: A Rejected Proposal:** How my future father-in-law's initial rejection of my request to marry his daughter became the template for my approach to creating value as an agent-advocate in commercial real estate.
- **Chapter 4: An Unlikely Process Geek:** If I can become a disciple of processes and checklists, so can you - how I use questionnaires, forms and repeatable processes as a roadmap to successful transactions, and greater creativity as a real estate thinker.
- **Chapter 5: Getting The Deal Done:** What sales and tenant representation look like when they're run by a true agent-advocate - someone with a commitment to client service and doing the right thing.
- **Chapter 6: Selling a 23,000-Seat White Elephant:** How selling an unwanted basketball arena showed me my true calling as a broker.

And here are the takeaways I hope to provide if you take the time to read my thoughts and ramblings:

- Real estate decisions can be complex, but **simple processes and methods** can add clarity and give the leaders responsible for the process confidence that they are meeting their objectives.
- How to **construct a mental framework** that allows you to make commercial real estate decisions based on sound information and experience.

- **How to demand that your real estate service providers (and future landlord) align their interests with yours** before you take a single step into the valley of the shadow of death (as I like to think of the current commercial real estate landscape).
- **The key questions to ask** that will ensure your broker performs proper due diligence.
- The Information Age has transformed commercial real estate - you need to know **how to sort and assess the flood of information** and use it to make decisions.
- **How to escape the McProcess Trap** that has ensnared so many mid-sized companies as commercial real estate leasing has been packaged as a commodity over the last 20 years.
- **The Three Ps** that allows Cardinal (and other well-run brokerages) to provide mid-sized businesses with a tailored real estate solution and representation that serves the client's fiduciary interests: Professionals, Processes, and Performance Pay.

I may have missed my Johnson O'Conner-dictated calling as a bus driver, but for the next few pages you can think of me as a tour guide. Let me show you around the present-day commercial real estate landscape - and also point you to a better place.

1.

A Better Way to Broker

It was 2005 and I was in my sixth year at Trammell Crow, the commercial real estate development firm where I had dreamed of working since I first decided I wanted to be in real estate. Known simply as "Crow" within the industry, it was a publicly-traded developer and commercial real estate service provider to the nation's largest firms. In its heyday, Crow was viewed as one of the nation's most interesting companies. Owning over 300 million square feet in commercial real estate, Fortune Magazine put the company's colorful founder, Fred Trammell Crow, in its U.S. Business Hall of Fame and numerous other national magazines featured the company and its leaders on their covers.

It was late on a Friday afternoon, and I was alone in our office with the Trammell Crow executive who handled our account with Bank of America. Crow was responsible for nearly all of BofA's real estate and more than 125 of us in Crow's Charlotte office were assigned to the hometown bank's account.

Led by then-CEO Ken Lewis, the successor to Hugh McColl Jr., Bank of America had gone all-in on Six Sigma, the set of tools and strategies designed to improve business and process quality and outcomes. Popularized by Jack Welch during his leadership of General Electric, Six Sigma was all the rage in the late 1990s and early 2000s and Lewis had led BofA on a deep dive.

At roughly the same time, Crow had won the contract to manage BofA's enormous real estate portfolio, swollen by the years of McColl-led acquisitions that had transformed little North Carolina National Bank into one of the nation's largest financial services firms.

Crow took responsibility for thousands of BofA ATMs, branches and critical data facilities, as well as high-profile tower construction plans in Charlotte, New York and beyond. To secure such an important contract, once-freewheeling Crow had agreed to spend hundreds of thousands of dollars developing and applying Six Sigma to the entire spectrum of commercial real estate. The Six Sigma consultants had come in and helped us build checklists and procedures for overseeing for the entire brokerage practice, build-outs, tenant improvements, new construction, asset management, lease administration, on and on. It was a little like trying to transplant the brain of a traffic cop into the body of a gunslinger.

That day had featured a BofA/Six Sigma crisis, and the Crow account executive, normally a man of high confidence, had spent hours on the phone. By late afternoon, he was visibly worn out from the bureaucratic handholding and arguments about quality and process management that had devoured his day.

The crisis was resolved for the moment and my buddy, the account exec, was feeling expansive. He turned to me and, by way of counterpoint to the Six Sigma Black Belts with whom he had spent the day sparring, said: "Culbertson, this Six Sigma stuff is for a bunch of wussies. You and I both know it: Commercial real estate is a gut business."

I laughed and agreed with him, but in my gut, I knew he was wrong. In fact, it struck me that the confidence that a checklist provides is exactly what was missing from commercial real estate brokerage.

There was an absence of rigor in the brokerage world that I had been exposed to. The account executives I knew at the firm rarely had any street experience and saw little connection between the efficiency and effectiveness of how they ran a transaction and how they were paid. They participated in the upside of their deals, and were insulated from any downside. As one of them once told me, "My job is great! All I have to do is play golf with CFOs!"

In the years before I joined Crow, I had worked for a company that developed warehouses; that experience reinforced my belief that we needed a new paradigm in brokerage - one that gave the broker some of the proverbial "skin in the game" and did a better job of aligning the interests of brokers and their clients. I had done deals across the country, and too many times I had seen deals go sideways, clients get left in the lurch and money and time get wasted because the broker, the person tasked with making the deal happen, neglected to pay attention to due diligence or failed to prepare for a negotiation.

As I went home from the office that night, my mind was racing with ideas about "a better way to broker." A short time later, I left Crow to start Cardinal specifically with the idea of building a brokerage firm around exactly the sort of alignment of interests, checklists, processes, procedures and intense attention to detail that Crow - and so many of our colleagues in commercial real estate - downplayed.

What BofA was trying to do with Crow by forcing Six Sigma down its throat, I would create on my own: a professional partner-agent whose interests would be aligned with those of the client.

Back at the beginning of my career, commercial real estate brokers still played a critical role as keepers and guardians of valuable market information. The best brokers knew - whether in their head or in well-kept files - where the available space was in a given market, who controlled it and what general terms the market would bear.

The Internet and the age of Big Data have changed all that forever. The same tools that allow homebuyers to sort online residential real estate databases and see what every person on a block or in a neighborhood paid for their home and when they paid it - a reality that has fundamentally altered the role of the residential broker - are widely available in the commercial real estate world. The commoditization of market data on the internet threatens to mercilessly disintermediate the traditional broker, who is no longer the keeper of the keys to the kingdom.

These days, any traditional broker who describes their primary role in a transaction as "knowing the market" is irrelevant. In an age of Information Overload, the broker's primary function has shifted from being a broker/"market maker" to serving as a client's advocate and guide through a complex transaction, with a laser focus on providing wise counsel. This new-style broker – what I will describe in this book as an "agent-advocate" – clarifies a client's needs and advocates relentlessly on behalf of the client all the way through a transaction. When I am compensated at the end of a transaction, my view is that I am being paid for my ability to provide clarity to a complex transaction.

This won't win me any industry Broker of the Year awards, but the reality is that traditional commercial real estate brokers share a set of traits that are particularly unhelpful for clients in the current environment. Here is my list of the most obvious problems in the commercial real estate brokerage game:

The classic "agency problem:" Traditional brokers operate under a compensation structure that motivates them to operate in their own best interest - not that of their client. I refer to brokers who are willing to sacrifice their near-term self-interest to benefit their client's best interest (with the knowledge of earning a fee, obtaining a referral, and future reciprocity) as "agent-advocates." Academics who have studied the dynamics involved in the classic agency problem call economic actors who are willing to sacrifice immediate self-interest "pro-social" - a term I will use a few times in this book.

Trusting their intuition: Traditional brokers are not analytical or data-focused. With a flood tide of data washing over them, few traditional brokers have the interest or skills to analyze the numbers and objectively interpret how they can be put to work on behalf of clients. Like the traditional baseball scouts in "Moneyball," determined to keep making gut-level decisions based on what their eyes tell them, they're being left behind.

The rugged individualist: Years of working in an "eat what you kill" environment has conditioned traditional brokers to operate as lone wolves. Such a broker struggles to assemble a team that can bring diverse skills to bear on a complex transaction, including something as simple as involving brokers in other markets where a client might need to lease space.

---

1 By using this term, I'm not saying traditional brokers are therefore "anti-social" - just that they operate under a different set of motivations that I believe make them less than ideal representatives for many clients.

> **Lack of formal training:** Professional development and skills training - which in most other industries would help professionals adapt to a changing environment - is almost non-existent in the industry (partly a function of the Lone Wolf Syndrome noted above).
>
> **"Slamming deals:"** Compensation structures and the nature of the industry motivate brokers to close deals as quickly as possible. That leaves little room for creative solutions, application of detailed problem-solving processes and proper due diligence.

To me, traditional brokering is an unrewarding profession. Clients are understandably suspicious of their brokers; many of them believe their broker is overcompensated for driving little, if any, value in the deal process

When I left Crow to start Cardinal Partners, it was to create a brokerage and consulting firm that would act as an extreme advocate on behalf of clients. I know we live in an era where "extreme" has become a jargon-y, marketing buzzword, designed to connote edginess and cool; I didn't pick it for that reason, but because client advocacy has taken a backseat in real estate for too long. Bullying clients into accepting bad deals in order to keep repeat customer landlords had become common in brokerage and I was determined to use processes and checklists, a different compensation structure and a patient, innovative, creative, problem-solving approach to transactions to stake out a position on the opposite end of the client-service spectrum.

I'll give you a typical example from the world of commercial real estate, working as a "tenant rep." Here, your job as a broker is to help the prospective tenant find space to lease. The conflict arises from the fact that as a broker, your financial incentive is to lock the tenant up in as long a lease as possible at as high a rent as possible and for as much space as possible (we'll talk about this more in Chapter 2).

When I'm interviewing to serve as a tenant rep, I always ask the prospective client if they've ever had a bad experience with a commercial real estate broker. Usually, this draws a polite smirk or a quick roll of the eyes, but one time recently the question provoked an over-the-top reaction from a usually-reserved executive: "Let me tell you what this SOB did to me!"

The executive and his broker were members of the same country club, and he had trusted the broker on that basis. Instead, the relationship turned into a nonstop battle over the broker's failure to negotiate competitive lease rates, negotiate for a lease termination option that the executive wanted (which can reduce a broker's fee by more than 50%) or assist in developing a sensible and efficient expansion plan for the fast-growing business.

The last straw came when the executive ran into his new landlord at the club's debutante ball – the landlord was a member too, of course – and the landlord immediately advised his tenant to get a new representative the next time around. Turned out this was the tenth deal in a year that the broker had completed with the landlord, an accomplishment that won him a trip to Vegas from the grateful landlord – and the eternal mistrust of his supposed client.

"Brokers," the bitter client told me, "are more crooked than politicians and attorneys!"

There is a very specific kind of client who gets screwed in deals like this. And it's not Bank of America or any other large corporation. Any company that's big enough to have its own in-house real estate department is generally savvy enough and commands enough business to dictate its own terms to the brokers (like BofA forcing Crow to jump through its Six Sigma hoops).

- It's the mature, mid-sized company with very specific real estate needs, where a single CFO or COO is tasked with figuring out the space problem (often in addition to staying on top of the books or coming up with an operational efficiency strategy).
- It's a family office or family-owned business. It's the growth-stage business that thinks it might needs to increase office space by 10x over the next three years, but with some flexibility to ramp up or down, depending on what the company's growth looks like.

These are companies with complicated needs and executives who want a real estate solution but don't have time to become experts in the field. Facility costs often are the largest or second-largest asset on the books, but (perhaps because it is everywhere) real estate is easy to take for granted. And managing a real estate transaction can be a nightmare, with a multitude of stakeholders, including employees, customers, investors, regulators and neighbors.

These companies - probably your company, if you've read this far - need brokers who will:

- **Clearly define expectations:** The best of the new breed of brokers work with their clients at the outset of a process to define goals, then adjust as the objectives inevitably shift.[2]
- **Agree to be "partners":** The client has to agree to share key information about facilities, business strategy and functions, and IT. The agent-advocate's focus must be not just on fees, but also on long-term goals like facility flexibility, cost reductions and employee satisfaction.
- **Structure a tailored process:** Like you, I hate checklists. They run entirely against my intuitive DNA. However, the reality is that a good checklist keeps you from making common, stupid mistakes. They free you from the worry that you might be forgetting something, allowing you to think creatively and make decisions with confidence.
- **Define key criteria and analytics:** These become the basis for making a final decision in a transaction.
- **Manage the transaction:** A well-run process will hit all key transactional benchmarks on the way to a streamlined, efficient close.
- **Behave like an agent-advocate:** The solution to the traditional agency problem lies in linking the agent's fee to the long-term success of the transaction. Long-term is the key word here: Do you want to hire a broker who is looking for short-term gains? Or do you

---

2   The longer I am in the business, the more I know to expect the unexpected in a deal. At the outset of a transaction, the client usually does not entirely know what he wants, which is why the "goal conversation" - what we at Cardinal call the DSQ (see Chapter 3) - has to happen early and often. That leads to a plan, but one that we expect to have to change on the fly. After all, in the words of the great philosopher Mike Tyson, "Everybody has a plan until I hit 'em."

want to find the agent-advocate who is focused on long-term relationships? For more on this, see the Appendix, along with the worksheets and examples at our website (www.goforbrokerbook.com).

We do all of these things at Cardinal Partners. We thrive on working with people to provide clarity to complex real estate transactions. We put money where our mouth is and use innovative consulting tools to provide an experience to our clients that they say they actually enjoy. We typically report to someone in the company's C suite or a top and trusted advisor and our transactions are almost always complex and involve some element of consulting. We are not the broker for an off-the-shelf, "just get it closed in a hurry" deal.

No one has ever gotten the problem with present-day brokerage services - and the differentiated product that we were offering - quite as well as a young technology entrepreneur I worked with a few years ago. He was the type of person I love to work with – he was a talented executive, a street fighter at heart who valued "straight-talk", not bureaucratic fog talk.

He was from the South and was full of down-home sayings and idioms. I had worked with his company since its infancy, but now I was on my own with Cardinal and we were competing with CB Richard Ellis and Colliers International to help the company expand its headquarters and lease large distribution centers in Charlotte and three other North American markets.

When it came time for us to pitch him, the executive plopped down in his seat and looked me in the eye.

"Look, Culbertson," he told me, "the problem with your industry is that I'm buying a pig in a poke. I have no way of knowing what's inside the bag you're selling me. You're telling me there's a pig in there, and I want to believe there is, but the only thing I know for sure is that the more I end up paying in rent, the more you make in commission!"

It was refreshing to have a potential client acknowledge the elephant (or pig, I guess) in the room. Within 30 minutes, he and I had established goals for the assignment that would have to be met for the Cardinal team to be paid. The result was a process that involved clear understandings about motivation and clear lines of communication about progress toward goals. We met all our targeted dates and came in well under our goals for the company's Year One occupancy costs. The entrepreneur, who started out from a position of suspicion, eventually became so comfortable with our management of the project that he delegated the relationship to the COO so that he could focus on other parts of the business.

Now, you may be like a lot of the clients I encounter, who tell me they just want to execute a single, simple transaction. They say they're fine hiring a lone-wolf hotshot - all they care about is getting this one deal done. Once, a few years back, after I had finished my pitch for an engagement, I had the president of a trucking company tell me, "I just need a broker to handle this deal - I don't need a goddamn MBA!" Years later, the building that guy wanted to sell is still sitting empty and unused.

Since starting Cardinal, I have come to believe that effective, new-style brokerage is really about defining long-term goals for a company and its real estate portfolio and building a relationship around those things. And I've learned three key metrics that define whether a transaction has been a success:

1. The client views us as someone who can guide them through a complex transaction.
2. The process has solved the problem of misaligned interests.
3. The client was able to make a final decision with confidence and emerge feeling that their transaction was a great experience.

In my opinion, that is a better way to broker.

Now, let's take a look at how we get to those outcomes.

2.

From Broker to Agent-Advocate

In the last chapter, we talked about the "pig in a poke" problem for real estate clients. One of the common complaints about brokers is that they promise the stars and the moon when wooing clients, but once the exclusive agreement is inked, the service leaves the client wanting more.

Clients may not be as colorful in naming the problem as my friend with the tech company was, but they have long sensed it. Since 1979, when Harris started polling Americans about the prestige in which they hold various occupations, real estate agents and brokers consistently have placed near the bottom of the list, down there with the likes of car salesmen and politicians. This is too bad, because it keeps a lot of talented people from considering the profession.

Matters weren't helped in 2005, when economics professor Steven Levitt and writer Stephen J. Dubner published their bestseller "Freakonomics." That book noted that studies had shown residential real estate agents tend to push clients to sell quickly rather than wait for a higher offer, but are willing to leave their own homes on the market longer to achieve a better sale price. The book was a huge bestseller, and it was not lost on me that the section that most people seemed to find most memorable was the one about the agency problem.

Levitt and Dubner's point had less to do with the inherent morality (or immorality) of the agents than with the misalignment of interests in real estate (and many other professions, including the law): the increase in the agent's commission generated by waiting for a higher price is unlikely to justify the additional labor and time involved in carrying the listing for another month or three.

Consider this example: You hire a broker to sell your property, which has been valued at $1 million. Within a week, she generates an offer of $950,000 - $50,000 less than the theoretical value. Your broker urges you to sell; the market is dismal, she says, and this may be as good as it gets.

The commission on the sale is 6%, or $57,000, which the broker is probably splitting two, three, and sometimes up to five different ways. If you hold out for a few more weeks or months, looking for that $1 million bid, she stands to gain maybe $3,000 (which, again, will have to be split). If she has read you correctly as someone who is willing to settle for "close enough" to $1 million, her interests are absolutely served by moving this one onto the books and getting on with life.

It gets even worse in the instance of a tenant representation assignment. These commercial real estate transactions, in which a broker is charged with finding rented space for a corporate client, are among the most lucrative for brokers - and are also the source of most complaints about broker commissions. Commissions are calculated as a percentage (usually between 4 percent and 6 percent) of total rent due under the lease and are paid by the landlord - half upon lease execution and half upon tenant occupancy.

The 5 percent commission on a five-year lease for 20,000 square feet at an annual rate of $20 per square foot is $100,000. Cut the term to three years and the rate to $18 per square foot and the commission drops nearly by half, to $54,000. So it's in your broker's interest to talk you into a lease with the longest possible term at the highest possible rent. Even though that represents a higher commission payment on the landlord's part, he is happy to pay it - he now has you under lease for five years!

Any free rent your new landlord throws in further reduces your broker's fee; if you insist on a termination option in the lease, it could result in a fee reduction or at the very least in payment of the fee being delayed until the termination period has expired.

Want to shop around for a better deal? If your broker is thinking about the short-term gain of a fee, and not the long-term interest of the relationship, he is not going to be happy about exploring new options. The faster a lease is executed, the faster he gets paid. And the likeliest outcome of your comparison-shopping is going to be lease terms that result in a smaller commission for him.

Twenty years ago, when I was starting out in the business, one of the first pieces of professional "wisdom" that I got from my broker-in-charge was this: "John, get your commission secured, then like being in a house on fire, jump-out the nearest window and move-on down the road."

Is it any wonder brokers get invited on so many golf, ski and shooting junkets by their buddies the commercial landlords?[3]

Negotiations with "friends," and people with whom you routinely do business with, presents problems. It is difficult not to offer information when asked for it by someone with whom you are friendly. Landlords frequently entertain brokers because they know that a tenant representative may feel morally bound to be truthful to any questions posed to them. They may feel obliged to volunteer information when a landlord asks a direct question. Research shows that negotiations between friends tend to be less

---

3 If you're a broker and you're still reading, don't throw the book down in disgust just yet; I address the good that the best brokers can do later in this chapter. My goal here is to get all the issues out on the table so that all of us in this business can start rebuilding trust with our clients.

creative than deals between strangers. I've watched too many brokers reach quick agreements with landlords whom they consider friends or longtime negotiating partners, instead of taking the time to explore how to strike a better deal for their clients.

In his book *Antifragile*, the author Nassim Nicholas Taleb discusses the agency problem from a slightly different perspective. To Taleb's way of thinking, the problem with brokers is that they don't have "skin in the game" in the same way that their clients do. Like an unethical defense attorney who pressures clients to cut plea bargains to clear his overloaded docket, the influence exercised by a broker has a much greater impact on his client than on himself. It's another way that misaligned interests do disservice to the client.

A few years ago, to dig deeper into what was wrong in my profession, I put a bunch of senior real estate executives from one of the nation's largest institutional tenants (with 1000s of locations that sum to more than 25MSF) in a room and asked them open-ended questions designed to get them to talk about the good, the bad and the ugly of the commercial real estate brokers they dealt with on a daily basis.

We didn't even have to buy them a round of drinks before they unleashed a barrage of complaints:

- Too many brokers aren't equipped with the skills and determination demanded in a complex financial negotiation.
- Too many brokers lack the tenacity or willingness to undertake the difficult task of grinding out a good deal for their clients.

- Brokers don't ask questions and, when they do, they don't listen to your answers.
- Brokers are too likely to work from the same limited playbook, lacking an ability to seek the sort of creative solutions that would demonstrate they take their profession seriously.
- The most damning quote came from the executive who said, "You could probably fit all the good brokers in the U.S. on the head of a pin!"

Why did these realities bother me enough that I decided to found my own agency and consciously seek a different way? I go back to my mom and dad and my conception of myself as a "real estate psychiatrist."

The client, in need of insight and guidance through a complex purchase or sale, hires the broker as a consultant. To assist in that process and to help us provide the best possible solution, we ask and expect our clients to expose not only their desires ("I want to lease space for $15 a square foot!"), but also their bottom-line needs ("$21 - and not a penny more!"). The client, by sharing information with the broker, hands over a lot of the control of the transaction. Part of the agreement, it seems to me, ought to be that the broker is not solely focused on the transaction at hand, but also on the bigger picture - long-term goals that provide savings and strategic advantage.

Now go back to the broker who sells her client on the quick $950,000 flip or the one who tells his client that he's not going to do better than a five-year lease at $20 per square foot, all in the interest of moving product through the pipeline. Isn't that a betrayal of trust? If I were your shrink, wouldn't you sue me for malpractice?

OK, enough doom and gloom. My chosen profession isn't going away, if only for the simple reason that almost any real estate negotiation more complicated than renting a studio apartment represents more brain damage than most people outside the business are willing to subject themselves to. Just ask any non-real estate professional who has ever had the bright idea of going head-to-head with a New York landlord about their office lease renewal. In any market, a tenant will get his hat handed to him by the landlord at lease renewal time, unless you have someone very experienced negotiating on your side.

Real estate should be a major strategy consideration for all but the most virtual of companies, yet executives with no background in real estate often rely on instinct or casual chatter when making major decisions in the realm. In my experience, having a competent agent-advocate on your side to provide you with real estate intelligence can reduce your occupancy costs by up to 15%.

But that's just a minimal standard, a reason to tolerate a broker's misaligned compensation structure. There actually are many additional professional services a strong broker can - and should - perform in a real estate transaction, but they require a re-imagining of the broker's role. Forget the notion of the broker as existing only to grease the transactional skids. Instead, start thinking of an "agent-advocate," a professional capable of performing the following functions:

Effective negotiation. Many clients don't have the desire or intestinal fortitude to battle effectively over crucial but arcane deal points. An agent-advocate who does so while strategically managing both sides through tough issues and getting to a win-win solution is a valuable asset. The result is confidence that you have a firm understanding of the deal, flexibility with your holdings and a great deal.

Due diligence management. For your traditional broker, focused exclusively on the one-time transaction fee, due diligence is something to be hurried through. But done properly and with attention to deadlines and details by an agent-advocate, due diligence gets deals done on the proper terms.

Real estate intelligence. Commercial real estate has become increasingly complex over the past decade. The best brokers add clarity to the morass of data by handling much of the analysis needed to make the decision that their clients need to get buy-in from all of the stakeholders. The agent-advocate saves your time and protects your confidence by providing clarity to today's complex transactions.

Process expertise. Six Sigma and a thousand different consulting firms have redefined how even the most soft skill-focused businesses think about process. Yet companies inexplicably continue to entrust one of their largest balance-sheet expenses - real estate - to inveterate hipshooters. A true agent-advocate gives her client deliverables that organize information and offer clarity about the best options, giving the client confidence that every detail is being covered and every possibility explored.

Team leadership. Many complex real estate transactions require input from third-party service providers, public officials, boards of directors and other constituencies. An agent-advocate with strong people skills and the ability to build networks around shared interests can be the difference between completing a deal for incentives for a plant relocation or watching that same deal run aground on the rocks of government vs. business mistrust. But how many brokers raised in the world of "eat what you kill" and Lone Ranger-style dealmaking are equipped for this kind of sandbox play?

The list of eight questions that follows is designed to sort the pretenders from the true agent-advocates. Now, obviously this list is a little self-serving. It reflects the values and priorities that I have built Cardinal around; I would expect my colleagues and myself to ace all these questions if someone came in and asked them of us.

That being said, I offer this list as an aid to anyone who wants to push a new paradigm on their broker/agent-advocate relationship. These are the hard questions that any and all individuals and companies with real estate needs should be asking of their real estate professionals.

1. **The Dan Sullivan Question®**: Credit here to Dan Sullivan, founder of the "Strategic Coach®" method of training entrepreneurs; our first question is adapted from one of Dan's core methods for teaching people to set goals and be effective in their lives.

   To test whether a firm's goals are aligned with yours and how seriously it is listening to your objectives, ask this question (I call it the DSQ, or "Dan Sullivan Question":

Assume that it is a year from now, and you and I are meeting right here to discuss the transaction that has occurred, what will have to have happened for you to feel good about your progress with this deal?

If the broker's answer doesn't encompass the goals and objectives you have outlined for your transaction, you're talking to the wrong person. At Cardinal, we have asked the question hundreds of times. We take the responses our clients give and make them a part of the Key Performance Indicators by which we are graded at the end of the deal.

2. **Are They Driven by Process, or Instinct?** Ask to see their "playbook." Ask for samples of deliverables from past transactions that you would hope to see during your transaction - things like market reports, financial projections and spreadsheets, analyses of terms. Ask to see due diligence checklists for leases, purchases and sale negotiations. If a broker can't provide basic process documents, you're likely dealing with a hipshooter who believes real estate is still a "gut" business.

   If they don't have a playbook, ask for examples of best practices.

3. **The Teamwork Test**: If you're being offered a team to work on your transaction, ask exactly what each member's area of expertise and responsibilities are. The team should feature a well-rounded mix of aptitudes that makes sense to you. If the transaction

involves real estate outside the local market, ask how the firm will handle out-of-market resources. Does the broker ever refer deals outside of their company or network? If not, why?

You want the top team working on your transaction, regardless of whose business cards they carry.

4. **Demonstrate Real Results**: How does your potential broker measure results? Ask this as an open-ended question and note carefully whether "client satisfaction" is mentioned. If you ask the potential broker how he or she will measure results in your transaction, is there any reference to your goals and objectives?

Next, drill down: What is the broker's plan for achieving your goals? How will you determine how much space you need? How will you find a buyer for your challenging asset? Will your assets be shopped to the usual suspects, or does your broker have some creative ideas about how to achieve your goals that come from outside the normal playbook?

5. **Are They Interested in Doing the Details?** Ask detailed questions that demand specific answers. Something like, "How can you help us reduce facility expenses?" or, "Tell me about a creative marketing strategy you have used to sell a distressed asset" should yield a set of specific answers and examples of how the broker has helped past clients achieve their goals. Their answers will give you a good idea

of whether the potential broker regards details as things that get in the way of the deal or critical steps that must be worked through regardless of the time it takes.

6. **Negotiation 101**: Drill down on negotiating tactics, skills and experience. Ask for an example of a situation where the broker's negotiating skills reversed a deal that was going down the tubes and turned it into a win. What are their goals in a negotiation? What training has the broker had in negotiating? If you are interviewing a large firm, ask how they will take steps to avoid conflicts of interest among clients.

7. **Listen & Learn**: As we saw during the real estate executive focus group, not being listened to is a top complaint of clients. Ask your potential broker if they survey their clients. How often? What are the results?

   After you're done with the interview, think back on the time the potential broker took with you and how respectful they were of your objectives and agenda for the meeting. If they weren't paying close attention, there's less than zero reason to think that will change once you're signed as a client.

8. **Will They Accept Pay for Performance?** Finally, we come to the bottom line: Is the firm willing to put its fee on the line for your satisfaction? Ask about the "pig in the poke" and address "the elephant in the

26

room" - the reality that the brokerage's interests aren't necessarily aligned with yours. Will they acknowledge that fact and discuss it without becoming defensive? Tell the potential broker that you expect some portion of their fee to be put at risk until you've met your objectives at the end of the transaction.

Anticipate pushback on this demand; national brokerage firms generally reserve this mechanism for their largest clients. But stick to your guns. To see a list of suggested mechanisms for linking fees to objectives both quantifiable and soft, visit the resources page on our website at: www.GoForBrokerBook. com. And watch closely how your potential broker acts when you open this avenue of negotiation; see what their behavior says about Point 6 above.

I've talked a lot about processes and Six Sigma so far. Now it's time to dig in and see where these things play a role in a complex real estate transaction. I've got some stories to share that will hopefully keep your eyes from glazing over, so let's get after it.

3.

A Rejected Proposal

It was snowing and my head was spinning as I backed my 1984 Volvo 240D clunker out of a St. Louis driveway in the winter of 1995. I had just been to visit my girlfriend's father, asking permission to marry his daughter.

His unequivocal answer: "No."

I was stunned and angry; that memory is still a tough one for me, even all these years later. Looking back on it from my current perspective as a father of three, I can see his point of view. I was a 25-year-old ski bum whose current base of operations was Vail. My politics were, to his mind, too liberal and I was certainly far too rough around the edges for his daughter.

But even as he shot me down, my girlfriend's father gave me an opening: a list of five hurdles to clear to win his blessing for our marriage.

- Get a (real) job
- Meet his mother
- Introduce him to my parents
- Explain how I planned to support his daughter in her accustomed lifestyle
- Buy a home in a real city (i.e., not a resort town)

Basically, if I wanted to marry Leslie, I would have to completely upend and remake my life. There's no doubt he fully expected me to drive back to Colorado, plow through a six-pack of Coors Light and disappear forever.

If he'd seen all those personality tests my mom put me through as a teenager, he might have done things differently. Because

I was one determined young man. Given a roadmap to marrying the woman I loved, I set to work. In short order, I moved home to Charlotte, took a job with a real estate developer and enrolled in a nighttime MBA program at Queens University.

I put my parents on a plane to St. Louis to meet Leslie's father. I went to Florida to meet Leslie's grandmother (a very kind woman who ended up being one of my greatest advocates).

And I bought my first house - an experience that brought me face to face with the agent-principal issue that I described in the last chapter. I interviewed three experienced brokers but couldn't figure out how to distinguish between their firms or their pitches for what sounded to me like a pure commodity service. Even more frustrating was my feeling that I didn't even really know what questions I was supposed to be asking. What answers could I demand that would somehow protect me against getting taken for a ride on the biggest purchase I had made in my life up until this point?

Finally, like so many others in my shoes, I threw up my hands and hired the broker I had known when I was growing up and whom I liked the best. The process I chose was as unsatisfying as the results.

When I went back to Leslie's dad to confirm that, yes, I had completed the Five Labors of Culbertson, and was ready to marry his daughter, he grudgingly acknowledged, "You're the most persistent person I've ever met." But he kept his word, and we were married - and remain so to this day.

Both experiences - with my neighbor-broker and with my father-in-law - were in the front of my mind more than a decade later, when I founded Cardinal Partners. I wanted to eliminate the black box of principal-agent conflict that had so baffled me in hiring a residential broker, so from Day One I put in place a value creation process for all our engagements. We have tweaked it along the way, but the result has been leadership, relationships and creativity on all of our assignments.

When talking about the future firm of Cardinal, often we say that we want Cardinal to provide clients with a Disney World experience. Traditional brokers leave clients feeling like they are "just another" client, while Cardinal clients invariably come away from the experience feeling that they were our only client - roughly the same difference between going to a "normal" amusement park and a Disney park. I particularly like this analogy because just like Disney, with their obsessive study and management of everything that goes into the customer experience, from ride wait times to bathroom placement and cleaning, we build our unique offering and client experience on a set of repeatable underlying processes and procedures.

The DSQ Conversation. Instead of starting with us, we begin with the client. We ask questions aimed at understanding a potential client's needs, unearthing the bottom-line goals of the project and identifying the likely obstacles to achieving a client's goals. The Dan Sullivan Question® ("DSQ") that I mentioned in the last chapter - the one about how we'll be able to look back on a transaction and define it as a success - is essential in this process. It helps us see the assignment through the other person's eyes - which is the first step in creating any value. Not only have we gained valuable information, we have formed a relationship by asking the right questions. By the end, we're able to outline the client's Dangers, Opportunities and Strengths.

Now, look - I know I said earlier that you ought to hire a broker who really listens and understands your problems, and this is clearly a part of that process. And I truly believe that a lot of the problem in my industry lies with brokers who have forgotten (or never understood in the first place) the fiduciary duty we owe our clients. So yes, I believe it's really important to <u>just listen</u> at the outset.

Here is the other thing about listening - great negotiators listen all of the time. They have an intense curiosity that probes for information and are constantly testing their assumptions. If the broker you are interviewing is too wrapped up in making a pitch or making a point to listen to you, you should wonder how effective he will be in representing your interests in a dynamic negotiation situation.

Harvard's Program on Negotiation cites the work of writer Malcolm Gladwell, who interviewed two Los Angeles police officers who had staked their own lives on their ability to read other people's intentions. One of the officers chose not to shoot a wide-eyed teenager who confronted him with a handgun. Something in the boy's face told the officer - correctly - that he was not really in danger. The other officer did not hesitate to shoot a man who was reaching into his overcoat as he approached his squad car. This officer sensed danger - again, correctly; that man was carrying an armed bomb.

Writing in *The New Yorker*, Gladwell said that while the two policemen were different in temperament and appearance, his conversations with them were surprisingly similar: "they never stopped watching, even when doing the talking ... [one of the officers] gave the impression that he was deeply interested in me. It wasn't empathy; it was a kind of powerful curiosity."

Friends and clients tell me I have that same kind of focused attentiveness and I've come to believe it's essential to being a good agent-advocate. When I go through the DSQ Conversation process, I'm not just acting as a sponge and hoping that you'll be impressed with what a good listener I am. I'm also deploying my curiosity because I'm deciding whether I want you as a client.

At Cardinal, we offer a customized, tailored solution to real estate needs. If you're executing a growth plan handed down from corporate that specifies that you must be in X location of Y size in Z zip code, then you may not be the right client for what we're doing. If you're a cookie-cutter client who only wants a cookie-cutter solution, Cardinal may not be the best fit. There are other firms that crank out those transactions one after another.

Our ideal client is one who wants to partner with us in a creative relationship. We do best when we're working for small-to-medium sized companies, often ones that are on a rapid growth trajectory and with a range of possibilities that demand flexible real estate options. Our clients are innovative, dynamic, exciting enterprises and we bring the same level of intensity to finding real estate solutions that they do to prosecuting their everyday business.

Obviously each engagement is unique, but one Danger we frequently identify through the DSQ process is keeping real estate-related processes from distracting a company from its day-to-day operations.

The flip side of that danger is the Opportunity provided by a new facility, sale, relocation or expansion. Particularly for relatively young companies, this is a chance to grow into a physical infrastructure that reinforces their developing corporate identity. New offices and facilities can energize employees and help attract new team members who are fired up about joining a company that's obviously headed in the right direction.

At the same time, we are careful not to prejudge Dangers and Opportunities. We put all our effort into understanding your point of view on your company and your industry, using your language, to get to the heart of how to add value and develop confidence in a transaction process.

Once we understand the client's Dangers, Opportunities and Strengths, we're in position to align our compensation with our client's success. This is where the R-Factor question I mentioned in the last chapter comes into play, in establishing our **Key Performance Indicators (KPIs)**: What indicators can we put around this transaction that will allow us to conclude whether it was successful one year from now, three years from now, five years from now? See an example in the Appendix and at www.GoForBrokerBook.com

Everyone on the Cardinal team knows the KPIs for each transaction, and we review and discuss them with the client regularly. Any adjustment to a transaction's KPIs is made only after input from the client.

A quick word about KPIs. We've found over the years that it's easy for a client to say "I want space for $16 a square foot, that should be my KPI." Then we get out into the market and he decides that the business really needs to be in a different location and it's worth it to pay $18 a square foot to be there. At that point, we need to either go back and agree to change the KPI or scrap it altogether.

I have heard a landowner say: "I want $200,000 per acre for my land! And that should be my KPI." That is well and good, but if the land is only worth $100,000 per acre, we have to either establish different expectations or decide not to take the assignment. This type of "honest expectations" conversation is critical if I, as an agent-advocate, am going to guarantee certain results. It's how I avoid falling into the traditional broker trap of taking a listing and then adjusting the client's expectations downward once the offers start coming in.

All that is simply to say that we try to be very careful - and realistic - when we peg our KPIs to hard numbers.

We also try to link our KPIs to more subjective judgments: Did you feel Cardinal was responsive to your needs as a client? Were your phone calls promptly returned? Did you feel as though we listened and incorporated your priorities into our efforts in a creative manner? Were we persistent enough?

These are less concrete than hard metrics, but they lead to **Value Creation Review™** conversations at key points in the transaction that are truly useful. See an example in the Appendix and at www.GoForBrokerBook.com. Our policy is that if we can't demonstrate adequate progress toward KPIs during a Value Creation Review, we refund meaningful portions of our fee.

Having drilled down to the base level of a client's goals, dangers and fears heading into a transaction and established what the KPIs will be, we respond with our proposal. This information package outlines what we heard from the client, our proposed solutions and the terms we propose for moving forward with the assignment.

In more than seven years of doing business this way, the only client who has ever questioned whether we hit our KPIs was an owner who listed his property for sale with us. He was so abusive and difficult to work with that after six months we were in the process of ending the listing and firing him when one of the prospects we had dug up during the process came back with an offer that ultimately proved acceptable. Despite pulling a proverbial rabbit out of the hat on that one, we ended up in a fight on fees ... which only strengthened my conviction that we had done the right thing in starting to fire the guy.

More common is the scenario where our willingness to put our fees at risk for our client's satisfaction wins us business that we shouldn't even be able to compete for - like with a major super-market chain that was making a big move into our market.

To many traditional brokers, the notion of working with KPIs hanging over your head will sound stressful. But I personally enjoy the knowledge that a transaction doesn't end with the signing of papers. Knowing that there is an ultimate reckoning to come, a final **Value Creation Review™** conversation to be had when everything has played out, keeps me focused on my transactions and working hard throughout the assignment. I always find those sort of "After-Action Review" conversations to be invaluable in offering lessons and perspectives that have made me a better agent-advocate.

I know for a fact many of my broker colleagues think the way I do business is nuts. Many of them actively dislike the way I talk about our profession; those guys have found plenty of ways to make their displeasure known over the years. But this is the only way I know to do business that brings the interests of broker and client into alignment. To build the trust that clients deserve, they must be able to follow the money and feel that I'm pulling in the same direction they are.

The question I get asked more than any other by colleagues and competitors is a variation on this one: "How can you take the chance that a client won't fairly value your work?"

My answer is relatively simple: The more time I've spent in this business, the more I find that leaving a little money on the table isn't the worst thing in the world. If a client feels you over performed and were underpaid, they're going to feel they got good value. That feeling will come back to you in repeat business, enthusiastic referrals and other ripple effects.

I have wagered my business on my conviction that, as the brokerage industry becomes more commoditized, this type of "pro-social" behavior will set Cardinal apart. More than half of our business comes from a small group of fans who like our approach and believe strongly in our thought leadership within the industry.

For the brokers who have read this far, let me ask a question: If clients finish a transaction feeling that they didn't get good value, or that you were overpaid for your performance (like so many of those real estate executives I interviewed for my focus group a few years ago), then don't we as an industry have to take a hard look at the value proposition we're offering?

As I wrap up this chapter, I want to go back to the story about asking my father-in-law for permission to marry Leslie. It's kind of a funny story to tell now, but it was a hard thing to take at the time. I was bitter at having to meet all those conditions and, despite the years that have passed, what went on in the mid-1990s has never really become a laughing matter for us.

But in looking back at my 20-year journey from rejected suitor to a husband and father of three (still working hard to support his wife in her accustomed lifestyle!), I give my father-in-law some credit. Not only did he kick me hard enough in the rear end to transform me from a ski bum to a successful business owner, but he also gave me my first and best lesson in how to build a better brokerage. On that snowy winter's afternoon in St. Louis, he was like the nightmare client. I wanted to talk about my Opportunities and Strengths, but all he saw were my Dangers. I wanted to close the deal then and there; he set sky-high KPIs that I had to rearrange my whole life to meet.

And in the end, I think we both would agree, we got to a win-win solution. And that brings me to my next topic: negotiations.

4.

An Unlikely Process Geek

Anyone who knows me knows that I'm among the world's least likely process geeks. As a kid, I knew plenty of guys who were in Boy Scouts, where the motto is "Be Prepared." I was more likely to be the kid throwing rocks at those Boy Scouts than doing anything to be prepared.[4]

I wasn't sitting in class studying; I was cutting class to go off-campus to the nearby 7-11 to buy candy and sell it to my classmates in the halls between classes. I got away with a lot because my father was a prominent businessman and member of the local school board. I must have been pretty good at it. I was told by the son of Diennie Crowell, the incredibly patient principal at Irwin Ave School where I attended, that one of the last things his mother said before dying was "John Culbertson! Sold Candy! In the hallways!"

I've already told you that at the age of 23, when I decided to get my act together in order to win permission to marry my girlfriend, I was little more than a ski bum, with all the lack of direction and drive that stereotype brings.

And even now, as a business owner, husband and father of three in his mid-40s, friends will tell you that when it comes to my mouth, I still hail from the school of "shoot first, ask questions later," capable of impulsive acts like volunteering to go on a church mission trip to Botswana before checking with my wife.

Sounds like the perfect fit for the cowboy real estate broker I've spent most of this book railing against, right?

---

4   And this is nothing against the Boy Scouts either. I may not have been one, but I've hired a number of Eagle Scouts over the years - former Scouts are a great fit for what I've built at Cardinal, which is a platform on which everything we do consistently and systematically creates value. My goal is to surround myself with people who are energized by that kind of work.

Except that's the exact opposite of how I've built Cardinal Real Estate Partners. I knew at the time I left Trammell Crow that I wanted to build a practice that was process-oriented and avoided the sloppiness and inefficiency that I saw all around me in the real estate business. That conviction was reinforced by a conversation I had shortly after starting Cardinal.

I was having breakfast with a friend of mine who was a boutique investment banker at McColl Partners. Charlotte is thick with boutique investment banks that serve many of the same mid-sized companies that I do, often as an advisor on the sale or recapitalization of these companies. Many of Charlotte's boutique investment banks are descended from a firm called Bowles Hollowell Conner that pioneered that kind of corporate advisory work in the 1980s and early 1990s.

At breakfast, my investment banker friend and I were talking about the recent sale of one of his competitors, Edgeview Partners, to CIT. The commercial finance giant from New York had come in and paid a big number to buy the bank, and he was shaking his head.

"It's amazing," he said, explaining that much of what made Bowles Hollowell unique was its attention to detail and process quality. The Bowles bankers and their descendants poured huge amounts of time and energy into writing in-depth marketing materials about their clients, then carefully followed a step-by-step process of creating a list of potential investors, contacting those investors and executing a rigorous auction process. Every junior analyst and mid-level associate who came in the door was taught the same playbook, until they could run the process in their sleep - which was not really a joke, given that many of those junior folks spent up to 18 hours a day in the office.

"Those guys are running the same playbook and checklists we did at Bowles, and they're fanatical about tracking everything," my friend said. "That's all it takes, and someone comes in and dumps a pile of money on the table."

The conversation reinforced my determination to soak in all I could about process expertise. I took the crash course in Six Sigma that I was given at Trammell Crow (and that most of my colleagues ignored) and supplemented it with study of the work of pioneering industrial statistician W. Edwards Deming, the American professor widely credited with helping spark the post-war Japanese industrial boom by teaching leaders of top Japanese industrial manufacturers the industrial process that became widely known as Total Quality Management.

I studied how the Deming approach to industrial manufacturing could be applied to businesses like mine, that deliver human services instead of widgets. As I said in the last chapter, I want Cardinal to be the "Disney World of commercial real estate brokerage" - not because I want people standing in long, mazelike lines to buy my listings, but because I want our underlying commitment to process, repetition and checklists to result in outcomes that feel as magical as a visit to the Magic Kingdom.

Deming boiled his work down into 14 essential points; it's #5 that's always spoken most powerfully to me: "Improve constantly and forever the system of production and service, to improve quality and productivity, and thus constantly decrease costs." This was closely related to Deming's "Plan-Do-Check-Act" cycle, in which he argued that manufacturers spent far too little time planning their work.

44

PLANNING IS KEY TO PROJECT COST CONTROL

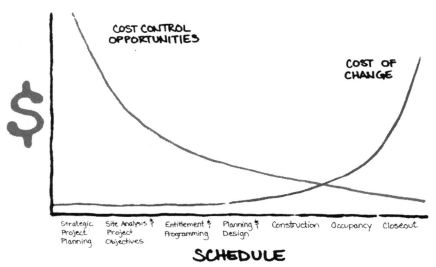

Invest your effort up front, Deming said, by improving the process to the point that all your parts and components are as nearly identical as possible and the improved results of your work efforts will more than compensate for the additional cost.

These concepts proved revolutionary in assembly line-manufacturing, fueling the Japanese automotive and electronics triumph over America in the 1960s and 1970s. And they apply equally to services businesses. As we've already discussed, the goal in traditional real estate brokerage is to get deals done as quickly and cheaply as possible. Planning and checking gets in the way of "slamming" deals.

Traditional brokers assume they understand the client's objectives - or care little about them in the first place. Clients are pigeonholed into categories - "tenant" or "buyer" or "seller" - and hustled through a process designed to get a deal done as

quickly as possible. Once the deal is signed, it's on to the next one.

Instead, I built my Cardinal practice on a foundation of practical tools that deliver the desired results with speed, effectiveness and consistency: questionnaires, worksheets, checklists and deliverables. Over time, my playbook has grown to resemble the one my investment banker buddies use to run their deals. In all, we have about 225 defined methods that we use for everything from onboarding a new client to answering the phone to paying a bill.

The result is the series of processes and methods that we call "The Better Way to Broker."

Checklists = Confidence
The Due Diligence 360™, for example, is 221 points long - designed to ensure upfront disclosure of all physical and capital issues with a property we are marketing, as well as any potential concerns around entitlement, planning, zoning, transit, utilities, adjacent owners and the environment. (See the example in the Appendix.)

Intentionality = Results
There's also a worksheet called Packaging The Hunch™ - we call it "PiTcH" - that we work through before placing an important call. The worksheet is designed make us think about why we are making the call and what has to happen during the call for it to be a success. (See the example in the Appendix.)

This sounds crazy, right? Why would you fill out a whole worksheet before you make a simple call? Here's the thing, though - it also turns out to be a great thing for busy people to go through before picking up the phone and dialing. The process of thinking through why I'm calling and what I hope to accomplish saves me time, because it reduces by about one-half the number of calls I make!

Friends = Referrals

We also have a worksheet for referrals. (See the example in the Appendix.) All of our business comes from referrals in one form or another, so we take them very seriously. When another broker refers a client to us, we want to make sure that client feels appreciated and that the broker who sent them our way is rewarded. I also am a big fan of referring clients to other brokers, or bringing other brokers onto our team to extend our reach or fill in specific, specialized skills needed for a transaction. I use referrals to ensure that I'm putting the best team to work on a transaction.

The traditional challenge around referrals in the real estate business has been that they often involve vague agreements and understandings about how fees will be split. That makes mistrust, suspicion and fee disputes the norm in the industry.

So we wrote a one-of-a-kind Cardinal Referral Program document, spelling out exactly how we split fees, down to describing the precise difference in the services Cardinal handles in a case where we're getting 20% to 40% of the fee vs. those we handle in a case where we're getting 50% to 65% of the fee.

As I wrote my playbook, I realized that the other place where I could benefit from discipline and process expertise was at the negotiating table. I had been at too many negotiating sessions where a single rash statement or ill-advised ploy had blown up transactions that should have been closed on mutually agreeable terms. Part of this was the gunslinger, lone-wolf mentality that was epidemic among traditional brokers, who like to play things fast and loose, allow their emotions to get the best of them and lose focus on the end goal of "getting to yes."

"Did I tell you that I went to Harvard?"

Getting To Yes, of course, is the title of the famous, late-1980s business bestseller written by the guys who started Harvard Law School's Program On Negotiation (PON). I've traveled on three separate occasions to Cambridge to take courses at the PON, hooked by course titles that spoke a language I was thrilled to hear after 20 years of being kicked around in commercial real estate: *"Dealing With Difficult People"*; *"The Art of Saying No"*; *"Bargaining With The Devil: When to say no, and when to walk away."*

I've learned a lot at Harvard and have met a lot of fascinating people, but by the time I started attending PON workshops, I was so steeped in Deming and Six Sigma that I was frustrated by the lack of checklists and worksheets.

So I came back home and used what I'd learned to create a worksheet we use on every assignment. We call it "**Prepared to Win-Win™**." The DSQ mentioned in Chapters 2 and 3 is part of the worksheet, but we also use it to gauge our assumptions about the other party's negotiating position. Before any important negotiation, we take the time to answer the questions in the worksheet, with the aim of thoroughly assessing the client's interests and our perception of the other side's interests. The worksheet helps to identify strong alternatives, generate novel proposals, and stimulate discussion at the table. (See the example in this book's Appendix or go to the Resources page at: www.cardinal-partners.com)

There is a three-step process to this worksheet.

1. Define what the client wants from the negotiation and what are the alternatives if there is no deal.
2. What are the other side's alternatives and how can we learn more about them?
3. Finally, we answer a series questions aimed to construct a persuasive argument that can be delivered with clarity and authority.

Always, always, always the goal is to create an atmosphere for negotiations that recognizes that the goal is not asymmetrical "victory" by one side (yours, of course) over the other but a "win-win" that recognizes and coordinates the needs and wants of seller and buyer, tenant and landlord, and manages the expectations of both parties to a common understanding of terms.

If you click through to the worksheet, you'll note that it includes a detailed list of communication tactics to look out for when negotiations are not going smoothly. Some of these are lessons I've learned the hard way, others were given to me by the Harvard guys; all of them are designed to avoid the problems that occur when a cowboy pulls a pistol at the negotiating table.

Company culture is often one source of problems. I spent nine months negotiating a lease between a notoriously tough corporation in the shipping and logistics space and a landlord who had an equal reputation for bare-knuckle tactics. As things developed, the lawyers for each side, predictably enough took a dislike to one another and began digging their heels in even more. Business became personal and that's always dangerous, as we all learned from *The Godfather*.

To me, this is the most treacherous negotiating scenario, because when aggressive attorneys get into fighting stance, it's easy for them to lose sight of what is really important to their clients in the fight over other deal points. A good lawyer looking for any advantage in a negotiation may grab hold of a negotiating point that really isn't of much importance to your client. Is that what you want an entire deal to break down over?

I generally let the attorneys run the show at the negotiating table on non-business points, but I always try to make sure to be in the room to keep an eye on what matters most to the client. Many brokers get the LOI "inked", hand over the final negotiations to the lawyers and cross their fingers that the deal will get across the finish line, but part of my obsession with process is being there to do what I can to keep things on track.

Some brokers operate from a default negotiating position of suspicion and aggression. Based in the South, I have cultural reasons for not preferring that style, but I also don't think it's an efficient way to claim value in a negotiation. Working for a landlord, I handled a 32,000-square-foot office lease deal where I worked with a Los Angeles-based broker who surprised me early on with an outburst that put me on my heels and allowed him to set some terms in his favor.

As the weeks and months rolled forward, though, I saw the broker use the same tactic repeatedly and it began to take a toll on our overall relationship. Annoyed, I started digging in and giving less than I would have if he had been easier to work with. A year into the lease, the tenant stopped paying rent and a legal battle began. The landlord and I remembered the jerk broker and were far less willing to mitigate the situation than we would have been otherwise.

Not all negotiating tactics need to be the equivalent of taking a deep breath and counting to 10 (though that's always a good practice when emotion threatens to override reason). Correctly deployed, some tactics can be quite aggressive, like low-balling the initial offer in cases where there's reason to believe money expectations are high or holding out until the last minute to negotiate an agreement when the other side is under time pressure.

In one recent negotiation, on behalf of a lessee with two years remaining on their office lease, I delivered a well-reasoned explanation of why we would be moving in 24 months if the group did not receive a rent reduction in the near term. We won generous concessions that will hopefully set the stage for a successful renewal negotiation in two years. Even if the client ends up moving, they have already begun making the case for why they need to make a change, which ought to make for smoother discussions in two years.

Ultimately, any negotiating tactic you deploy should be in service of a larger battle plan. What is your end goal, what is your best alternative and how does playing a particular card at this time advance you toward those two endpoints?

All these forms, questionnaires and checklists sound painful and they sometimes are, but there's also a secret to them: they make me a more creative agent-advocate. A great process and a detailed checklist that lays out the roadmap to that process keeps me on task and prevents forgetting key steps in a transaction. I don't have to reinvent the wheel for the transaction, because I have the process laid out for me.

That frees me to be more thoughtful about the details and structure of each transaction. Instead of worrying about nagging details that I may or may not have forgotten, I can step back and think about the big picture. Cardinal is a small shop, with a handful of clients, but our back office processes - and, more importantly, our efficiency - outstrip those of any mega-brokerage I have ever encountered. That let's me compete for and win brokering challenges that normally would be unthinkable for a firm of our size and frees me to be as creative as I can in executing those challenges.[5]

Let me give you tell you a story that illustrates how our commitment to process and upfront due diligence pays dividends. In 2007, I was hired by Bowater, the timber and newsprint giant, to help sell a number of its key developable timber tracts in the face of declining demand for newsprint. One of those

---

5 Here's another secret about the checklists that relates to my earlier comment about how I hire people at Cardinal: They make it a whole lot easier to hire and train transaction managers. My junior folks execute the playbook, which makes real estate transaction execution into grown-up version of a connect-the-dots puzzle. All I do is recruit young men and women who are smart, can execute and stay on task, and who have a passion for learning the business. This doesn't mean they don't make the same mistakes everyone does, but the checklists give them a guide to show them how to change their process so they don't repeat those mistakes. With those tools, I am able to run my business and manage my junior transaction managers in an apprenticing style that is relatively uncommon these days.

assignments was the sale of the beautiful, 6,156-acre Aetna Mountain tract, just outside Chattanooga, Tenn.

I was driving the property one early spring morning, checking-off items from the **Due Diligence 360™** checklist, when I encountered a 2-acre area where there was literally steam rising from cracks in the ground. Trees had dropped into sinkholes, where they were turning into charcoal.

When I got back in cell range, I called the Bowater folks and told them what I had seen. Yes, they said, that's a fire in an abandoned underground coalmine; they're actually pretty common.

The Bowater executives suggested that I ignore the issue and deal with it if and when it came up in due diligence. But experience told me that would be the wrong time to handle it. Better to get out in front of the problem, frame it as something to which there was an existing solution and avoid having it derail us at the end.

We hired ARCADIS, a leading national engineering firm, to assess the problem and define a solution, which ended up amounting to a cost of about $100,000. We were up-front about the underground fire and how to fix it and ended up actually incorporating the site into our property tours for potential investors, jokingly referring to the area as the "weenie-roasting pit" (the property was being marketed for resort development).

The ultimate buyer of the property was a highly sophisticated private equity land fund. I can tell you with confidence that, had we tried to hide the ball, not only would they have found out about the fire, they also would have sat on that knowledge until the final days or hours before closing, when they would have tried to re-trade for a multi-million-dollar purchase price reduction. Instead, the deal closed on time and without any re-trades.

The Due Diligence 360™ ensures that the frustrations and surprises that often derail transactions are minimized. A New York developer who was buying land from a client of ours once commented that we provided the best due diligence package he had ever seen. He added that his company typically closed only about 50% of the deals that they put under contract, usually because of undisclosed issues that they discovered in their due diligence process. If all brokers followed our 221-point checklist, he said, their closing rate would be 100%.

The final place where process rules my work is in how I try to think about Cardinal's progress as a business. My friend Dan Sullivan at Strategic Coach taught me what he calls the "Experience Transformer®" technique. It's a simple practice of asking yourself four questions about an experience. We have a form for this too (of course) and hardly a day goes by that I don't complete a couple of them, whether in the aftermath of a negotiation, a closing or a simple, routine meeting.

1. What went well in this experience?
2. What didn't?
3. Knowing what you know now, what would you have done differently?
4. What steps are to be put into place to assure that the experience does not/does happen again?

I can hear my former Trammell Crow colleague right now: "John, we both know this is a gut business. No amount of checklists and questionnaires are going to guarantee that every deal closes."

And he's right. Sometimes you run the entire playbook, do everything right, try all your different negotiating tactics and nothing works. The deal falls apart. But that's the nature of this business and of almost any professional services business. When dealing with human beings, there are no guaranteed outcomes. I wouldn't be in this business if I weren't comfortable with accepting reasonable risk.

What separates the successful from the merely competent is the determination and ability to reduce those risks as much as possible. If your broker can't demonstrate a commitment to process that goes beyond, "Trust me, I know what I'm doing," you're not getting the service you're paying for.

5.

Getting The Deal Done

At Cardinal Partners, most of our transactions fall into one of two broad categories:

1. A facility location selection process with extensive due diligence that we call **The Strategic Tenant Advocate**™. It is a comprehensive process that results in justifiable decisions when a facility is part of our client's core business strategy.
2. A process of streamlining the sale of complex real estate we call the **Comprehensive Asset Sale**™. We treat each assignment uniquely and implement a focused strategy that coordinates all communication, engages the most likely buyers and provides control and accountability.

Having given you a sense of the thinking behind how we use process and checklists to manage our client work, I want to walk you through what each of these processes looks like when they're run by Cardinal. Even if you're never going to hire us, I encourage you to use this chapter as a guide when talking to your broker of choice about their service to you. If you're not getting this level of advocacy and engagement from your agent, you might want to think about hitting the reset button on the relationship.

I also want to comment here on the interplay between owning and developing your own property vs. leasing it. In my practice, I encounter many companies outside the real estate business serving as their own landlords and owning what I view as too much risk.

In today's economic environment, which puts such a premium on corporate agility, I believe flexibility around real estate needs is far more important than having the proverbial stake in the ground. Companies that develop their own real estate very rarely achieve returns that are comparable to independent entrepreneurs and development professionals, primarily because most of those companies' core competency lies outside real estate and because when push comes to shove they must answer to different corporate priorities than the highest or best use of a piece of property.

Imagine a fast-growing data center business in Northern Virginia. The business has become a colocation provider of choice for a shared server provider to cloud-based software businesses; business is booming. The owner decides to build a Taj Mahal headquarters that announces to the community that this business has arrived and is a major player. He has plenty of cash on hand to buy the land and build to spec, and look how much cheaper his mortgage is going to be than paying rent on the current facility!

Construction proceeds on schedule. There's some scope creep as the facility is modified for the company. No thought is given to who the next tenant to use this building might be, because it's being custom-built for the owner.

The building is complete, the headquarters is beautiful, the local newspaper comes out to cover the grand opening and the owner's announcement that he'll add 50 jobs at the site.

But within three years, the market changes. A series of successful cyberattacks on collocation facilities sends companies seeking ultimate online security to hardened server facilities run by a consortium of the government and the new "fortified Internet" providers.

The company has tied up a bunch of cash in its building, which is now obsolete. In order to move his business to where the revenue now resides, the owner is forced to sell the building - which is customized for a now-obsolete business model - at a substantial loss, instead of simply paying to get out of a lease with a landlord or allowing its term to expire.

We refer to this as the "true cost of occupancy" and it's important to quantify. Sure, you will pay a bit more for a lease than you would for a mortgage, but you also are capable of negotiating termination, expansion and renewal options that give your company the ability to nimbly adapt to changing circumstances. Own only the critical real estate that you must control to keep your business going.

The Strategic Tenant Advocate™

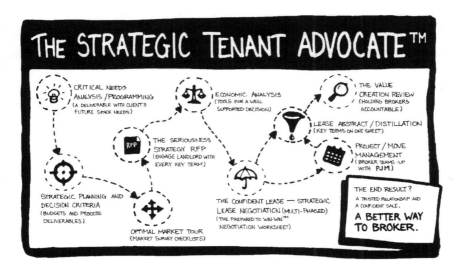

Our goal here is finding our client a lease that will support the company's business strategy for the duration of the lease.

Of nearly equal importance is giving the client clarity into the transaction. Leases are complex and real estate is frequently a company's second- or third-largest expense. Despite that reality, as I've already noted, most of the companies we serve don't devote a full-time executive to real estate matters. Corporate moves, relocations, lease negotiations and facility additions or renovations generally fall to the CFO or COO to handle.

The result for the executive charged with overseeing a move or facility addition is a classic "black box" problem. Money goes into the black box and a new headquarters, manufacturing facility or branch office comes out, but what goes on inside the box just makes your head hurt to think about.

Our goal as agent-advocate is to use our processes to make that black box as transparent as possible. Through a thorough selection process, extensive due diligence on targets, thoughtful negotiating and clear communication about decision-making, we aim to deliver the right space and the right place on the right terms for our clients.

The best outcome from a **Strategic Tenant Advocate™** process is a client who can clearly explain why the space they ended up with and the terms they settled on were the right choice for their company at this stage of its growth.

Here are the steps we use to accomplish that.

1. Client Critical Needs Analysis™
   Our first conversation is about your business, not ours. What are its current needs? What do you anticipate for growth over the next three to five years? What are the downside risks in your business, and how much flexibility do you need in your growth plan? What KPIs are we going to use to measure success in this engagement? Clients get a program of the current and future space needs completed by our architects working in conjunction with our project team.

2. Strategic Planning and Decision Criteria
   This is where we really dig in. Here, we meet with all the key decision makers on the project and map out the steps of our process and what resources we will leverage to make informed decisions. Our analysts map a company's existing and future needs and we run a budget analysis to see whether relocation or a lease renewal is the preferred option.

3. Optimal Market Tour
   Considering both hard factors (like zoning and facility requirements) and softer ones (does your business need to be in the downtown financial district or does it feel a little more offbeat?), we map a strategy for touring potential sites and come up with an assessment of lease options. All this work is documented in our Market Survey Checklist.

4. Seriousness Strategy RFP

   This is the request for proposal that draws together all your priorities and key lease terms and communicates them to the marketplace. This is a critical table-setter for a successful lease negotiation. It is here where the relationships are created with the landlord for long-term success. Every concession, business term and innovative deal structure you need to meet your KPIs are requested with a tenor of assertiveness that tells the landlord that we are serious about our needs.

5. The Economic Analysis

   Here we use sophisticated in-house and third party lease proposal analysis tools to make apples-to-apples comparisons of all proposed leases. We make a recommendation and at the same time give the client the tools to make a well thought out decision.

6. The Confident Lease Negotiation

   As described in Chapter 4, we oversee the lease negotiation process, including working with attorneys, implementing the negotiating tactics described earlier. By using the Prepared to Win-Win, the goal is always to negotiate a lease that will work as well for the client in the final year as it does in the first year and that will support the business's opportunities while offering a hedge against downside risk. Our fee is at risk - so we "pull out all of the stops" to win for you!

7. Project/Move Management

   Most brokers drop out of sight after the lease is signed, but we have aligned ourselves with top project managers and architects to ensure that the vision that we mapped during the leasing process is seen through to reality.

8. Lease Abstract/Distillation
   All our clients are provided with a lease abstract that consolidates all key terms and conditions on a single page and can be enormously helpful when disagreements arise with landlords.

9. The Value Creation Review™
   This is the key final step in our process, where we ask clients to review our performance in comparison to the KPIs we established back at the beginning of the engagement. Often, our compensation is tied to whether or not the client believes we have satisfied the KPIs we set back at the beginning. As I've said earlier, this opportunity for us to identify ways to improve and serve you better in the future is one of the core reasons why I'm in this business.

The Comprehensive Asset Sale

With the bottom-line nature of most sales, clarity is usually less of an issue for sellers than for lessees. Satisfaction is usually a simple question of whether you got your number or not.

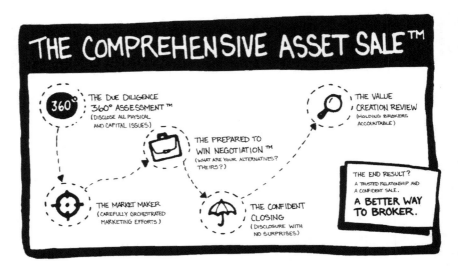

Here, Cardinal's commitment to process aims to engage the most likely buyers, coordinate all communication with them, streamline the sales process and give control to the seller and accountability on the part of the broker throughout the process.

1. DD360 Assessment™

   Completion of our 221-point Due Diligence check-list gives us into the DOS - Dangers, Opportunities and Strengths - associated with a client's assets. The checklist is designed to reveal all potential issues around entitlement, the environment, zoning, tran-sit, utilities and adjacent property owners. During this stage, we're also sitting down with key stake-holders in the sale to set our KPIs. See the Cardinal website for a sample of the checklist. www.cardinal-partners.com/resources

2. Market Maker™

   Every Cardinal marketing process is carefully orches-trated to maximize the appeal of the asset to poten-tial buyers, while at the same time setting the stage for a successful win-win negotiation. Our buyer lists are carefully thought out and we work hard to create a vision for your asset that will resonate at an emo-tional level with potential buyers, including carefully orchestrated tours. As we start to get offers, we keep in close communication with our clients about our progress.

3. Prepared to Win Negotiation™

   We use our Prepared to Win^2 Worksheet™ to set the stage for a successful negotiation that respects the wants and needs of the client and the poten-tial buyer. Communication is key at this stage, to make sure both sides have a common understand-ing of terms and remain on track toward a mutual agreement. See the Cardinal Partners website for a

sample of the Prepared to Win-Win worksheet (www.
cardinal-partners.com/resources)

4. The Confident Closing™
Here's where the attention paid to detail and process
in the first three phases pays off, as Cardinal coordinates documentation, final due diligence, reme-
diation and other pre-closing activities. The DD360
Assessment™ done at the start of the transaction
should minimize unpleasant late surprises.

5. The Value Creation Review™
No Cardinal engagement is complete until we have
finished our Value Creation Review, looking back at
the KPIs and whether we hit them. That allows us to
figure out where we could have done better and how
to improve in the future. See the Cardinal Partners
website for a sample of the Value Creation Review
checklist (www.cardinal-partners.com/resources)

6.

Selling A 23,000-Seat White Elephant

**For Sale
17-year-old obsolete basketball arena on 154 acres of land.
Includes 23,000 seats, 8 luxury suites and
extensive political baggage.**

Back in the late 1980s and early 1990s, the Charlotte Coliseum was the hottest ticket in my hometown. The NBA's Hornets were the first team from one of the four major professional sports leagues to call Charlotte home, and the city embraced them, selling out more than 350 consecutive games at the Coliseum. Hornets home games were the place in Charlotte to see and be seen.

By the turn of the century, though, the story had changed. The Coliseum, built on the city's western perimeter, almost five miles from downtown, was completed just before a new economic model for arenas, predicated on corporate luxury suites and city center locations, took hold in the NBA; it was almost instantly obsolete. In the late '90s, the Hornets' owner-ship started agitating for a new, downtown arena to replace their barely-a-decade-old home court.

It was poor timing - the NFL's Carolina Panthers were the new, hot young thing in town, having started play in 1995. The NBA's popularity was down in the post-Michael Jordan era and the Hornets were beset by a series of scandals small and large.

In 2001, the city's voters soundly rejected a non-binding referendum on whether to build a new downtown arena. The Hornets moved to New Orleans the following year (later to become the Pelicans), but the NBA agreed to give Charlotte a second chance, promising an expansion team for 2004-05 - if the city went ahead and built the team a downtown arena.

The city council went for the deal, proceeding with construction of Charlotte Bobcats Arena and reaping a backlash from angry voters. By the fall of 2005, the second-year Bobcats were starting play at the new downtown arena, the Coliseum stood empty. I got a call at my desk at Trammell Crow, where I was a senior vice president.

Was I interested in handling the sale of Charlotte Coliseum property?

As political hot potatoes went, this one was plenty steamy. The Coliseum may have been functionally obsolete, but the facility itself was still in good shape. There was no question about leaving it intact, as it would have competed for the concerts, circus visits and other events that were supposed to fill the new downtown arena on non-Bobcats dates. But for the many voters who had opposed construction of the new arena on the grounds that it was a waste of public money, tearing down a perfectly workable old arena was equally appalling.

As part of the political machinations and corporate arm-twisting that went into building the new arena, the real estate development arm of Charlotte-based Duke Energy, Crescent Resources, had agreed to pay $24 million for the Coliseum property - if it was rezoned to allow development of mid-rise office buildings. But when the city started looking at a rezoning that would open the site to more than 6 million square feet of office space, the planning staff and neighborhood groups on Charlotte's west side pushed back, saying development of a traditional suburban office park would do little to advance the city's economic and developmental goals for the relatively low-income side of the City.

Changing the zoning in early 2004 to allow the Coliseum to be redeveloped as a mixed-use project (which included strict limits on how much office space could be included in the project) caused Crescent Resources to drop its opening bid for the property from $24 million to $16.5 million - a $7.5 million shortfall in money that already was earmarked to help pay for the new downtown arena.

Meanwhile, state law required that the Coliseum, which was publicly owned, be sold through a competitive upset-bid process. For a broker, this was a significant twist. There would be no backroom deals - everything was out in the open and the City would announce all the bids. You couldn't hide behind vague statements about how much interest there was or wasn't in the property or who might be willing to go to $25 million if a potential buyer didn't put a higher bid in first.

City officials spent 18 months in 2004 and 2005 unsuccessfully trying to generate interest - and a higher bid than Crescent's revised bid - for the rezoned site. It was mid-2005 by the time they came to me at Trammell Crow to ask if we were interested in listing and marketing the property.

My Trammell colleagues thought the assignment was too risky and complex and opposed taking it on. I went ahead and put forward a proposal anyway, proposing the sort of at-risk commission structure I would later build Cardinal around: Trammell Crow would only make a commission on the deal if the net proceeds exceeded Crescent's $16.5 million standing offer.

To assure city officials I could handle sensitive negotiation with potential buyers of a politically charged property, I developed a prototype of the Prepared To Win-Win™ worksheet that I shared with you earlier. There would be no cowboys in the room when I sold the Coliseum - just me, making sure we got to a close. That worksheet, as simple as it is, helped me win the deal.

We pulled out all the stops for the marketing process, treating it more like a sale run by my friends in the investment banking world than a traditional listing. We developed a specific marketing strategy for the property and distributed over 2,000 marketing flyers to real estate development firms, generating 100s expressions of interest. We set up an online data room (another investment banking standby) to facilitate due diligence on the property and keep prospective bidders up to date on the upset-bid process.

The Coliseum process was the inspiration to habitually use two tools - - the " VOTA-SUCCESS®" and the Comprehensive Asset Sale™. VOTA is another Dan Sullivan tool and stands for Vision, Opposition, Transformation and Action, which are the four steps I walk clients through when we're thinking about how to go to market with an asset sale:

What is the **Vision** for the asset?

What are the likely sources of **Opposition** to a sale?

How can this asset be **Transformed**, thereby making it more attractive to potential buyers?

What are the **Actions** we need to take to maximize the chances of success in a sale?

The SUCCESS acronym comes from the powerful and fun to read book *Made to Stick* by the Heath brothers. We use this formula to help package complex real estate that result in a message that is:

Simple - usually one sentence

Unexpected - people remember surprises

Concrete - the facts are important

Credible - make the claim believable

Emotional – make the claim matter to the buyer

Story - I am from the South and we like to tell stories that make our claims hard to forget

The Comprehensive Asset Sale™, as I explained in Chapter 5, is how I streamline sales in a comprehensive process that leaves no potential buyers untouched and manages all the nagging details of a real estate transaction in an efficient and thorough manner. The first deliverable of this process is called the **Due Diligence 360™**, which with its 221 point due diligence checklist, can get voluminous, however, our clients tell us that they truly appreciate the VOTA SUCCESS component of the document and how we provide solutions to obstacles that they share with us.

Two development firms emerged as being the most interested in the Coliseum: Comstock Partners of Reston, Virginia., and Pope & Land Enterprises of Atlanta. Unlike Crescent, which had been almost solely focused on office development, both liked the site for its mixed-use development possibilities. Nearby amenities such as a public golf course, Charlotte's hub airport and a regional farmer's market enhanced the appeal for a live-work-play community.

Both groups made it known they would be willing to raise their bids if the site could be rezoned to allow even denser mixed-use development. But the political need for transparency and a completely above-board sale process made any quid pro quos with the city unthinkable. As broker for the deal, I shuttled back and forth between the buyers and city officials, facilitating meetings and conversations among the many stakeholders in the process.

I managed communication between the prospective buyers, the staff of the city's planning department and elected officials who were watching the sale process closely. Always, always, always we made it clear that no bids would be accepted that were contingent on a rezoning of the property; at the same time, I was able to manage communications between the potential buyers and the city officials so as to give both Comstock and Pope & Land comfort that the city was sufficiently invested in redeveloping the site to move forward with a rezoning once the sale was complete.

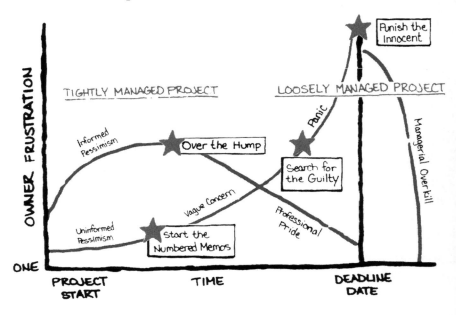

Remember that Prepared to Win-Win™ worksheet that won me the transaction? As things heated up with Comstock and Pope & Land, I had dozens of those worksheets spilling out of every file folder in my briefcase as I ran around town and worked the phones, trying to keep on top of the multi-track negotiations. My goal - and a lot of my value add in this transaction - was channeling all communication between the two potential buyers and the city through me. Because of the need for transparency, there were to be no one-offs or what the lawyers call *ex parte* communications; everything said to one buyer had to be said to both.

We all know that the more people involved in a decision, the harder it is to get to a resolution. A good friend taught me this simple formula for calculating just how quickly it gets harder: n x (n-1) / 2, where n equals the number of people involved in the decision.

That formula tells you how many connections there are to be managed within your decision-making group - 3 within a 3-person working group, 6 if you add a fourth, 10 if it's five people. By the time you get to a dozen people at the table, there are 66 connections to manage to keep everyone on the same page!

Savvy dealmakers know that the best way to get a deal done in that situation is to work at the edges - work one connection to get inside information, take that and leverage it to get on the same page with the guy on the other side you've identified as the final decision maker, maybe plant misinformation with a third person who you believe to be communicating with your competitor, and so on.

By inserting myself in the middle and insisting that everything go through me (and using my trusted worksheet to manage the discussions), I aimed to stand in the way of any one-offs and edge working. It was "honest brokering" in its truest sense and even as I sifted through my P2WW worksheets and labored to keep everything on track, I knew that I had found my calling and could build a practice around just this sort of representation.

We launched the upset-bid process in November of 2005 and it went like this: every time someone submitted a bid, it was published in a local newspaper. Prospective buyers then had 10 days to top the established bid by at least 5%.

Comstock started things with a $17.82 million bid and got a sigh of relief from me, since I had staked our commission on topping the $16.5 million Crescent offer. Pope & Land immediately jumped that, going to $19 million, and Comstock came right back with a $20 million bid.

There were three more rounds of bidding before Comstock finally dropped out and Pope & Land bought the property for $23.35 million - a 46% increase over Crescent's revised bid! The transaction closed in March 2006.

The Coliseum was demolished in 2007 and in early 2008 Pope & Land was successful in winning a city rezoning of the property to accommodate a $624 million urban town center development dubbed "City Park," which was to include 350 hotel rooms, over 200,000 square feet of retail, 400,000 square feet of office space and 1,750 residential units.[6]

Two professors from UNC Charlotte's Center for Real Estate later studied the Coliseum sale and wrote a teaching case study

---

6 This, of course, was right before the Great Recession hit and stalled redevelopment of the site. As of Summer 2013, the first vertical development was underway.

on it, noting that participants uniformly described it as "an overwhelming success from the public sector's perspective. "(The) disposition process was unusually non-controversial in light of the asset's size and value."

The Coliseum sale was the last major transaction I closed at Trammell Crow before leaving to start Cardinal and it was transformational in forming my notion that there might be a "better way to broker" out there.

Earlier in this book, I mentioned the concept of being "pro-social" - an economic actor who is willing to sacrifice his or her immediate self-interest (i.e., fee payment) for the sake of getting a better deal for a client or even an outcome that represents a gain for both sides in a deal. Academics who have studied how deals get done have concluded that agents with a pro-social outlook tend to get better all-around outcomes for all parties in transactions than agents focused narrowly on maximizing their near-term fees. As I told you earlier, I also believe there are long-term benefits for an agent-advocate who takes such an approach, in the form of repeat clients and word-of-mouth business that transcends short-term gains and make it worthwhile to leave the proverbial "money on the table."

Leading the sale of the Charlotte Coliseum, more than any other transaction in my career, made it clear to me that I was just such a "pro-social" broker. I thrived in my role as the middleman between the city and the potential buyers of Coliseum property; every morning during the months we worked on that deal, I awoke excited and motivated to do what I could that day to get all the parties closer to a win-win for everyone - a maximization of the city taxpayers' return on an important piece of public property and a huge piece of developable real estate that Comstock or Pope & Land could use to remake an entire region of my hometown.

Why am I this way? Well, all those tests my mom made me take back in the day would tell you that I was wired from the very start to do this kind of work - a "real estate psychologist," as I put it back in the Introduction.

But it was more than that. As I noted earlier, my dad's work as a successful wealth manager gave me a close-up view of the importance of fiduciary responsibility to clients. Dad's deep sense of fairness and equity didn't stop when he left the office, either. My father had a long track record of public service and was a leader on the local School Board during integration. When Charlotte desegregated its schools in the late 1960's and early 1970s, he was one of a handful of leading citizens who made a statement by keeping his children in the public schools and not sending them to the new private schools founded in response to a federal judge's busing order.

My mother got the public service itch and became the City's first female Chair of the Planning and Zoning Committee, breaking the tradition of developers in that role which had turned it into a good ol' boys club.

Politics and policy was often the topic of choice at the dinner table and we all had an appreciation for the power of Government. The eldest, my brother Ewell, anchors the left end of the spectrum - he is a successful organic orchardist in Colorado. My sister Ruth Samuelson anchored the right end of the political spectrum. My sister Laura and I got good at being between the two dodging pots and pans thrown from the ends and adding levity whenever possible.

Ruth went on to a long public service career in both local and state government and is now a leader in the state legislature; I decided to tilt at the windmills of commercial real estate by building a brokerage firm around pro-social values. In both cases, it's hard not to think our parents' commitment to doing the right thing set each of us on our respective paths.

As we move into my final chapter, where I will present you with some concluding thoughts, I want to keep the idea of "pro-social" behavior front and center. I believe it's key to solving some of the gravest problems we face as an economy and a culture.

Conclusion

You might think, as we wind down, that I have something against my fellow brokers. I've said a lot of nasty things about their work, cast aspersions on their motivations and stopped just short of calling your average, everyday commercial real estate broker "anti-social."

But it's really not personal. I feel this way about a lot of folks offering professional services these days. The same trend toward commoditization and corporatization that has been so broadly decried in retailing (the "Wal-Marting of America" is the most common meme for this) has taken place in our professional services industries, but with much less fanfare.

Yes, the economic collapse of 2008 produced a brief moment of national introspection about whether banks that were "too big to fail" were a good idea and whether corporate gigantism had contributed to a "big short" perpetrated on the American people, but that passed quickly. Five years on, it doesn't feel to me like much changed in the wake of the biggest American economic crisis in 80 years.

The truth of the matter is that there are many excellent brokers who do a great service for their clients. Many of them are among my closest friends and I work with often through associations I belong such as the Counselors for Real Estate (CRE); Certified Commercial Investment Members (CCIM); and the Society of Industrial and Office Realtors (SIOR). These uber-brokers love the game of real estate and play it to win. They have amazing amounts of energy and they love their clients. There is no doubt about it, you are better off with one of these brokers than doing it alone.

Law firms, banks, insurance companies, accounting firms, other financial services firms, real estate brokerages continue to merge in ever-larger combinations, chasing "economies of scale," "organizational efficiencies" and "synergistic returns."[7] What's lost in so many of these combinations is the personalization that, in my opinion, makes all the difference in a professional service relationship.

At almost any mega-firm, clients inevitably become commodities, as corporate bureaucracy insulates brokers, lawyers and other agents from the direct impact of their service.[8] At a super-sized, multi-office brokerage, law firm or accounting firm, an individual professional is less beholden to a list of specific, satisfied clients than to a revenue generation number that will determine commissions and year-end bonuses.

This has created a market opportunity. I specifically position Cardinal in opposition to the mega-brokerage experience. The CBREs and Jones Lang LaSalle's of the world are giant bureaucracies. There is little innovation happening in the brokerage ranks in firms like that, which are focused solely on serving the needs of their fellow Fortune 500 giants and maximizing shareholder returns. Lacking a pro-social agenda, firms like that will always be misaligned with the interests of small to medium sized firms.

---

7   My former firm, Trammell Crow, itself was absorbed into CBRE Group, now the world's largest commercial real estate services firm in a merger that closed in December 2006.

8   While it might seem like an unintended consequence of corporate mergers and growth, this insulating effect is in fact quite intentional - the larger a firm's client base and reach, the more insulated it is from the individual impact of one client's satisfaction or dissatisfaction. It's a rule of thumb in mergers at all sizes that high levels of customer concentration are a bad thing.

By contrast, my firm, Cardinal, focuses on vision, creativity and courage to make good things happen for its clients, rather than to try to squeeze every last dime out of them.

The key is, I'm not trying to win everyone over. At several points in this book, I've made the point that I'm not the right broker for every client and that not every client is right for my practice. But I have my "groupies," my raving fans and I am driven by a belief that I will be more successful in the long run through my service and loyalty to this small fan base than by trying to please everyone.

I'll say this as well, from personal experience - clients aren't the only people being done a disservice by the commoditization of professional services. So too are the very brokers, lawyers, accountants and bankers caught up in the mega-firm machines. Too many men and women of my generation, well-educated and well-paid though we may be, are not living up to their true potential by spending their work lives in unsatisfying, repetitive or unchallenging positions that serve the needs of organizations that have become far too large to be effective.

Me? Like my dad, now in his 80's and still working away, I plan to be plugging away at what I love until I'm 100 years old or they cart my corpse away from my desk - whichever comes first.

As an adult, I realize in retrospect that much of my checkered academic history was due to the fact that I suffered from ADHD in an era before that was an accepted diagnosis. Back in the 1970s, kids like me were "hyper" or "a handful" or "underachievers."

I struggled through and, in a world that comes at me quickly and often threatens to overwhelm me, I've now spent more than four decades learning how to make things simpler and more straightforward. I love my checklists and worksheets and firmly believe they result in better outcomes for my clients, but they're also the best (maybe the only) way for me to stay on top of something as complex as your typical commercial real estate transaction.

When I worked, at the beginning of my career, for International Airport Centers, the firm put me on a small development team in charge of warehouse developments on the fringes of airports like BOS, LAX, SEA and JFK - places that were on the front lines of the global shift to multi-modal transportation systems and just-in-time supply chains that marked the 1990s. A preppy Southern kid, I was dropped into some of the toughest real estate markets in the country and told to pull off deals that felt more like street fights than negotiations. I got a self-taught graduate degree in how to avoid being the sucker in a real estate deal

Those experiences have left me skeptical of anything taught in classrooms. That's why I'd rather hire a kid from a low-profile MBA or real estate program and teach him or her how to actually execute a real estate transaction on the job than go fishing for hotshots from prestigious B Schools. That's why if you gave me a magic wand, I'd try to bring us back to a world of professional apprenticeships, where tradecraft and professional wisdom were passed on in an on-the-job setting, in mentoring relationships that had real weight to them (as opposed to the postmodern, corporate idea of arranged mentorships, which generate about as many positive outcomes as a typical Internet dating service).

At Cardinal Partners we have a track record of successfully working with interns that have turned into apprentices. To see how we do it, checkout our white paper on internships on our website's resources section www.cardinal-partners.com

I will leave you with what I view as the four key principles of how my business is run - and how any professional services firm should be run. If you have read all the way through and think that I can help you with your real estate needs, I encourage you to get in touch by phone or through the Cardinal website.

If you want to pick my brain about other professional service providers who I think are giving similar types of service to what I do at Cardinal Partners, I'm happy to talk about that as well. And if you have your own professional services firm and are smart enough to see the need for change, I urge you to put these principles into practice at your own business.

1. Communicate early and often
2. Put your money where your mouth is and work to align your interests with your clients.
3. Use clear, well-designed tools, checklists and processes to provide clarity for our clients and advocate for their interests.
4. Perform rigorous due diligence in all that you do.
5. Be willing to try new approaches when old ones are not working.

Appendix
Resources and Tools

There are white papers, due diligence checklists, broker customer satisfaction scorecards and much more free information
at our website: www.cardinal-partners.com/resources

88

Prepared to Win-Win™

Commercial Real Estate Negotiation Worksheet

Before any important negotiation, take time to answer the following questions. A thorough assessment of your interests, and that of the other party's, will help you in identifying strong alternatives, generate novel proposals, and stimulate discussion at the table.

There is a three step process to this worksheet. First, define what the client wants from the negotiation and what are the alternatives (BATNA). Then ask yourself what the other party needs and how you may learn more about it. Finally, answer the questions at the end to exercise your problem solving skills, and to construct persuasive and articulate arguments that are delivered with clarity and authority.

Our Side (Yellow Paper):   Version 1 Date: ___/___/___

The Other Side (Pink Paper):   Version 2 Date: ___/___/___

Negotiation Preparer: Version 3 Date: ___/___/___

Step 1 of 3: What Do We Want?

1.1   Assume that the negotiation is over, the deal is done, and you are looking back over your progress - what would have had to happen for you to feel good about your progress?

Action Items & Notes:

Go For Broker

Step 1 of 3: What do we want? (continued)

1.2 What are our advantages, weaknesses, and vulnerabilities in this negotiation?

Advantages:

1.

2.

3.

Weaknesses and Vulnerabilities :

1.

2.

3.

1.3 From working with the other side up to this point, what have I learned about effectively working with the other side?

1.

2.

3.

Action Items & Notes:

90

1.4 Positioning our proposal with concrete data: What objective benchmarks, criteria, and precedents will support our preferred proposal? (market lease rates, comparables, NOI calculation methods, cap rates, demand information, third party reports, etc.)

    1.

    2.

    3.

1.5 How to keep your objectivity in the negotiation - improve your fallback option: What is my Best Alternative to a Negotiated Agreement ("BATNA")? - What are you going to do if there is no deal? What is *PLAN B*?

1.6 What steps can I take to strengthen my BATNA? What can you do to make *PLAN B* more desirable?

	%

Go For Broker

Step 1 of 3: What do we want? (continued)

Action Items & Notes:

92

2.1   What do we think the other side wants from this negotiation?

1.

2.

3.

2.2   What is the hierarchy of the other side? In what order should I approach the other side?

1.

2.

3.

Action Items & Notes:

Go For Broker

Step 2 of 3: Confirm our Assumptions about "The Other Side" (continued)

CARDINAL
REAL ESTATE PARTNERS, LLC

2.3 What do we think is the other side's "BATNA"? What are their options if they do not do a deal with us?

2.4 How can we find out more about their options? Evaluate the effective strength of our option to their *PLAN B*. Is what they have said consistent with what we feel is their *PLAN B*?

Action Items & Notes:

94

Step 3 of 3: Create value by trading resources, preferences, risk tolerance and deadlines

3.1   What is our relationship history? How might our relationship affect talks?

3.2   What parties not yet involved might also value an agreement?

3.3   Am I watching out for the common pitfalls that I typically fall into?

☐   Have I taken the time to be prepared?

☐   Have I reviewed all my notes and due diligence?

☐   Am I self monitoring my reliance on my intuition?

☐   Have I checked all the facts?

☐   Have I been too quick to trust the other side?

At Cardinal, we steer away from moves that could compromise values and weaken reputations if exposed. However, you should be aware when others use these ploys:

- **The Silent Treatment:** places burden of further negotiations on the other side.
- **Low-Balling:** if you sense the other side has high money expectations, put a low offer on the table.
- **Power of Print:** send the concrete data to the other side in writing.
- **Good Guy / Bad Guy:** one is reasonable while the other will not give an inch, e.g. stating one is constrained by management.
- **Leaving Money on the Table:** giving the other side more than he or she expected.
- **Fait Accompli:** suggest that a majority of the work is already accomplished and promise to settle up after.
- **Making the Other Party Clarify and Justify His Position:** best defense against an opening move.
- **Listing Pros and Cons of the Other Party's Position:** good move to create open discussion.
- **The Power of Guilt:** "Everyone else does it my way, what is wrong with you?" - an appeal to emotions.
- **Summary of Facts, Statements, and Agreements:** work to make a written summary whenever possible if breaking for the day.
- **Bluffs:** must be credible.
- **There are Times When Deals Cannot be Made:** give full statement as to why and maintain credibility.
- **Split Down the Middle:** keep in mind a 50/50 split is not always fair.
- **It's Too Complicated, Let's Make it Simple:** explain and understand step by step.

Go For Broker

**Step 3 of 3: Create value by trading resources, prefer-
ences, risk tolerance and deadlines (continued)**

3.4 How to Package a Powerful Message in Negotiation: go back and review the work sheet,
paying particular attention to the action items and notes you made.

Simplicity: What is the single most important thing to remember?

Find something unexpected to emphasize your point: What is the most surprising
fact to support your simple message above?

Have concrete information at your finger tips: The data must support your simple
message.

Find common ground that everyone can agree on: You will build credibility by
establishing facts they know supports your position.

Be passionate and emotional: What crucial life issue is at stake?

Everyone loves a story in a real estate negotiation: What is the best story that
supports your position?

CARDINAL
REAL ESTATE PARTNERS, LLC

Customer Referral Program*

Referral Mission Statement

Cardinal is serious about careful, intentional growth with clients. You can expect that we will treat any referral with the same care that we have treated you. Our goal is to identify friends and colleagues who agree to establish a meeting between Cardinal and a potential Cardinal client, simply based on the friendship, trust or respect that exists in your relationship with the prospect.

Cardinal Real Estate Partners, LLC ("Cardinal Partners") wants to encourage actively licensed real estate brokers and agents to leverage their contacts by making referrals to Cardinal Partners. We have found that the single largest obstacle in referring someone is the vague nature of how the referral source will be compensated. The following is the recommendation from Cardinal Partners for guidelines, compensation, roles, responsibilities, and how to resolve disputes. The guidelines have been structured with corporate clients in mind with a wide range of different services and product types taking place in local and non-local markets. The guidelines are not anticipated to cover every possible situation that can arise; however, the spirit of these guidelines should prevail in all situations.

The Referral Source

In order to participate in any referral transaction; the referral source must have an active real estate license. If the referral source or the referred company does not utilize Cardinal Partners, Cardinal Partners will receive no compensation.

Simple Referrals

A simple referral is a phone call, email, or written referral where the referral source does not have a written or oral exclusive and the company does not already have a broker.

10% to 15% of Cardinal Partners' gross commissions or net fees to the referral source and 90% to 85% to Cardinal Partners; such gross commissions to be determined in accordance with standard commercial brokerage policies including deducting any client rebate(s) and deal expenses or other splits with supporting third-party brokerage firms.

Exclusive Representations

Exclusive representation is when the referral source has a written exclusive signed by the contact covering the referred assignment specifically or all transactions in general. Oral or handshake exclusives also apply however, it is assumed that at some point a letter affirming representation will need to be produced and presented to a landlord and/or their representatives.

Go For Broker

Exclusive Representations Cont.

When Cardinal's gross commissions are more than $5,000 and;

Scope of services is generally as follows:

Referral Source	*Cardinal Partners*
Obtain Written Exclusive	Broker of Record
General Customer Coordination	Provide Market Survey
Definition of Requirement	Property Tours
RFP Coordination with Customer	Local RFP Coordination
Final Decision on Vendors	Local Vendor Coordination
Proposal and Lease Negotiation	Local Proposals, Leases
Customer Satisfaction Survey	Punch List and Satisfaction Survey

Under this scenario, the referral office remains involved in the transaction, but generally is not required to travel to the market. Commission splits are as follows:

35% - 50% to Procuring Office   *65% - 50% to Cardinal Partners*

Scope of services is generally as follows:

Referral Source	*Cardinal Partners*
Obtaining Written Exclusive	Broker of Record
General Customer Coordination	Provide Market Survey
Definition of Requirement	Possibly be Available for Tours
Property Tours	& Local Meetings
RFP Coordination	
Vendor Coordination	
Proposal Processing	
Lease Processing	
Punch List	
Customer Survey	

Under this scenario, the customer requests or requires that the referral source have a higher level of involvement in the transaction, including traveling to the market, conducting tours, soliciting RFP's, etc. Since the exact scope is difficult to determine (depending on the customer) the commission split is negotiable within the following parameters:

60% - 80% to Procuring Office   *40% - 20% to Cardinal Partners*

When Cardinal's gross commissions are less than or equal to $5,000; Commission splits are negotiable based on the involvement and requirements of the people and transaction. The referral source is encouraged to concede the great majority of the compensation to Cardinal Partners as these small transactions generally are not very desirable even when receiving 100% of the fee. You should rationalize this by paying fairly for execution of a non-desirable assignment, as they will be assured that their contract will be well taken care of and receive an excellent value. Often in the instance of a negligible referral amount, Cardinal Partners will make a contribution to a charity in the name of the referral source.

If There is a Dispute

All referrals must be registered. In situations where the parties cannot agree and the terms are defined as being "negotiable" herein; the issue will be settled through The Counselors of Real Estate ("CRE") arbitration process as provided for at the following site: http://www.cre.org/dispute_resolution/standard-clauses.cfm. The decision of the committee will be final – no appeals, end arounds, or bellyaching.

200 South Tryon Street | Suite 850 | Charlotte, NC 29202 | T: 704.953.5500 | www.cardinal-partners.com

Key Performance Indicators
Client Evaluation Form

This form is intended to assess the performance of the Cardinal Real Estate Partners, LLC ("Cardinal") tenant representative during the recently completed project for Client.

Client Manager: Name   Cardinal Representative: Name

Project Location: Address   Company: Name

Please use the following scale to rate the performance of the Cardinal tenant representative:

1 – Poor;   2 – Fair;   3 – Good;   4 – Very Good;   5 – Excellent

1. How successful was the Cardinal representative in understanding Client's requirement?   1 2 3 4 5

2. How thorough was the Cardinal representative?   1 2 3 4 5

3. How accessible was the Cardinal representative?   1 2 3 4 5

4. How effective was the Cardinal representative in securing the best possible lease terms for Client?   1 2 3 4 5

5. How effective was Cardinal in coordinating the project and in providing a communications link between the Cardinal representative and Client?   1 2 3 4 5

6. Overall rating?   1 2 3 4 5

Go For Broker

The Comprehensive Asset Sale™
Project _____ Check List

SECTION 1: General Information		
1.01	Ownership	
1.02	Street Address:	
1.03	County/State/Zip:	
1.04	Site Acreage:	
1.05	Tax Parcel ID	
1.06	Proposed Use:	
1.07	Proposed Closing Date:	

SECTION 2: Site Description		
2.01	Property Description	
2.02	Site Access & Adjacent Roadways	
2.03	Surrounding Development	
2.04	Adjacent Property Use/Zoning	
	a. North:	
	b. South:	
	c. East:	
	d. West:	
2.05	Narrative - developments occurring in the area	
	a. Residential	
	b. Entertainment	
	c. Commercial	
	d. Other	
2.06	Site Groundcover Characteristics	
2.07	Drainage & Site Slope Characteristics	
	a. Suspected Wetlands?	
	b. Locate:	
2.08	Visible Utilities	
2.09	Features:	
	a. Locate Wells on Map:	
	b. Protected Species:	

	c. Describe Other Wildlife:	
	d. Large Trees on Map:	
	Species:	
	(century trees, registered)	
	e. Rock Location:	
	Type/Features:	
	f. Waterways:	
	Streams/Creeks:	

SECTION 3: Title / Survey Matters		
3.01	Ownership Legal Entity:	
3.02	Provide Tax Maps	
3.03	Obtain Copy of Deed:	
	a. Dated	
	b. Type	
3.04	Obtain Title Company	
	a. Date of Report:	
	b. Title Rep? time/cost	
3.05	Exceptions/Restrictions:	
3.06	Prior Uses:	
3.07	Environmental References	
	a. EPA	
	b. DENR	
3.08	Title Requirements:	
3.09	Survey/Existing	
3.10	Survey Contract	
3.11	Final Survey	
	a. ALTA? time/cost	
3.12	Legal Description:	
3.13	Easements:	
3.14	Condemnations (Specify)	
3.15	Citations (U.S., State, Local)	
3.16	Archeology Reports:	
3.17	Research Site History:	

SECTION 4: Site Report

Go For Broker

CARDINAL
REAL ESTATE PARTNERS, LLC

Project _____
The Due Diligence 360° Assessment™

4.01	Environmental Site Assessment:	
	a. Describe any Evidence of Hazardous Materials:	
	Soil/Groundwater Contaminants:	
	Time/Cost Estimate:	
	b. Environmental Phase I	
	c. Environmental Phase II	
	Describe Scope of Required Mitigation	
	d. EPA Contact	
	e. Identify Other Environmental Agencies or Groups	
4.02	Wetlands/Waterways/Streams/Sheds & FEMA	
	a. Wetlands:	
	Deliniation:	
	b. Flood Plain delineation completed?	
	Are there areas that do flood?	
	SWIM Buffer:	
	FEMA Panel:	
	Date	
	Community Flood:	
	c. Water Shed:	
	Regulated	
	d. Water Mgmt District Contact	
4.03	Geotechnical	
	a. Obtain Engineer:	
	Report Date:	
	b. Soil Type(s):	
	c. Soil Problems:	
	d. Cost:	
	e. Earthquake Zones:	
4.04	Existing Structures	
	a. Number of Structures:	
	Size:	
	b. Demolition Required:	

		Cost:	
		c. Building Contaminants:	
		Cost:	
		d. Cemetery:	
		Locate:	
4.05	Existing Bldg Conditions		
		a. Architectural Plans:	
		b. Leases & Abstracts:	
		c. CAM Expense Information:	
		d. Insurance Expense Information:	
4.06	Current Property Taxes:		
		City	
		County	
4.07	Other: Neighborhood Association		
		BMP, CCR, POA	
4.08	Off-Site Concerns:		
		Narrative:	
4.09	Appraisal:		

SECTION 5: Development Requirements		
5.01	Zoning Official:	
5.02	Plat	
5.03	Planning and Zoning	
	a. Current Zoning:	
	b. Required Zoning?	
	Anticipated timing:	
	c. Variance Required?	
	Anticipated timing:	
5.04	Site Plan Review	
5.05	Building Permit	
5.06	Other Governmental Requirements and Procedures	
5.07	Building Code Official:	
5.08	Building Codes Jurisdictions:	
	a. Building:	
	b. Plumbing:	

Go For Broker

	c. Mechanical:	
	d. Gas:	
	e. Electric	
5.09	City/County Engineer:	
5.10	Storm Water, Erosion Control, Water Quality	
	a. Current Location / Capacity:	
	b. Site Storage Required?	
	c. Proposed System:	
	d. Storm Water Mgmt. System/Contact:	
	e. Fees/Calculation:	
5.11	Fire:	
5.12	Vehicular/Traffic Regulations	
	a. Name of Traffic Consultant (if any):	
	b. Dept. of Transportation Contact:	
	c. Traffic Counts on Area Thoroughfares:	
	d. Proposed Future Traffic Controls in Vicinity:	
	e. Proposed Roadway Widening in Immediate Vicinity (if any):	
	f. Proposed Medial & Curb Cuts:	
	g. DOT Drive/Encumbrance Permits in Place. Are any suggested?	
	h. Incentive programs:	
5.15	Approval Process Summary	

Project _____
The Due Diligence 360° Assessment™

SECTION 6: Site Restrictions		
6.01	Architectural and Design Standards	
6.02	Buffers/Screening Requirements:	
6.03	Development Covenants, Conditions and Restrictions	
6.04	Fire Protection	
6.05	Floor-to-Area Ratios:	
6.06	Height Restrictions	
6.07	Highway	
6.08	Historic	
6.09	Impervious Coverage:	
6.10	Landscaping	
6.11	Lighting	
6.12	Lot Coverage	
6.13	Parking	
6.14	Setbacks	
6.15	Signage	
6.16	Site Paving	
6.17	Utilities	
6.18	Other Ordinances (Specify)	

SECTION 7: Fees & Assessments (Indicate N/A if applicable)		
7.01	Identify Property Assessor Contact:	
7.02	Impact Fees Regulations:	
7.03	Building Fees (excludes utilities) Regulations:	
7.04	Traffic Fees Regulations:	
7.05	Fire/Police Impact Fee Regulations:	
7.06	School Impact Fee Regulations:	
7.07	Library Impact Fee Regulations:	
7.08	Parks/Recreation Impact Fee Regulations:	
7.09	Proffers:	

SECTION 8: Utilities		
8.01	Sanitary Sewer	
	a. Current Location/Capacity:	
	b. Proposed System:	
	c. Utility Company/Contact:	
	d. Fees/Calculation	
	e. Can it be assumed the land percolates?	
8.02	Domestic Water:	
	a. Current Location/Capacity:	
	b. Proposed System:	
	c. Flow Test:	
	d. Utility Company/Contact:	
	e. Fees/Calculation:	
8.03	Fire Protection:	
	a. Current Location/Capacity:	
	b. Proposed System:	
	c. Flow Test:	
	d. Utility Company/Contact:	
	e. Fees/Calculation:	
8.04	Natural Gas:	
	a. Current Location/Capacity:	
	b. Proposed System:	
	c. Utility Company/Contact:	
	d. Fees/Calculation:	
8.05	Electric:	
	a. Current Location/Capacity:	
	b. Proposed System:	
	c. Utility	

		Company/Contact:	
	d.	Fees/Calculation:	
8.06	Telephone:		
	a.	Current Location/Capacity:	
	b.	Proposed System:	
	c.	Utility Company/Contact:	
	d.	Fees/Calculation:	
8.07	Cable:		
	a.	Current Location/Capacity:	
	b.	Proposed System:	
	c.	Utility Company/Contact:	
	d.	Fees/Calculation:	
8.08	Other Utilities (Fiber):		
	a.	Current Location/Capacity:	
	b.	Proposed System:	
	c.	Utility Company/Contact:	
	d.	Fees/Calculation:	

Sources

"The Least (Prestigious) Jobs in America," Best Article Every Day, August 2009, [Based on results from 2009 Harris Interactive Poll).

"Real Estate Brokers/Agents Have an Image Problem," Jonathan J. Miller, Matrix: Interpreting the Real Estate Economy, August 2009.

"How to Build a Better Office," Jane Hodges, Copyright © 2007 CNET Networks, Inc. Focus Group, Cardinal Real Estate Partners, LLC, Spring 2010.

Industry Overview: Commercial Real Estate Brokerage and Management, Hoovers, 2010.

The US Department of Labor, Bureau of Labor Statistics, 2010, tracks 123,000 employees in the real estate broker business, and the National Association of Realtors claims 9.72 of It's membership is commercial.

The Real Estate Investment Trust Industry in the United States, ibid.

"Real Estate, the Most Imperfect Asset," Sarah Jane Johnston, Harvard Business School Working Knowledge, August 2004.

"Realtors weather the commercial real estate market," National Association of Realtors,
Marketwire, September 23, 2009; and Realtors.org.

"Why you can't trust a real estate agent," Paul Michael, Wise Bread, April 5, 2007.

The Dan Sullivan Question by Dan Sullivan. The Strategic Coach Inc., 2009. www.strategiccoach.com

"Leadership in Real Estate," National Association of Industrial and Office Properties (NAIOP) and Spencer Stuart, blue paper, 2003.

Acknowledgements

I would like to thank the employees at Cardinal Real Estate Partners, LLC, especially Matt MacCaughelty. I would also like to thank Tim Whitmire for keeping me from turning this into my "Jerry McQuire" manifesto. Thank you Kerry Hall for your fine editing. Thank you Dan Sullivan and Lee Brower for your inspiration and coaching. Thank you Robert Lapp – you are one fine intern.

I want to say thank you to my wife, Leslie, for allowing me to tell the rejected proposal story. I promise that I will never mention it to Hordy again.

Finally, this book is dedicated to my three sons: McRae, Luke and Julian. Remember; always be loving, generous, kind, faithful, brave and strong.

THANK YOU
FOR READING
THIS BOOK!

I truly hope that this book has helped you in some way. The world of commercial real estate has become increasingly complex and a great broker can add lot clarity to the decisions that any leader must make about facilities.

I would love to hear from you. If you have a story to share, or if you want to see if there is a fit between Cardinal Real Estate Partners and your firm, please reach-out to me at any of the following addresses.

Twitter: #CardinalsChirps
Twitter: #GoForBroker
LinkedIn: https://www.linkedin.com/in/johnculbertson
www.GoForBrokerBook.com
www.Cardinal-Partners.com
jculbertson@cardinal-partners.com

About Cardinal Real Estate Partners

Cardinal Real Estate Partners are brokers and consultants that think differently. Determined to be an advocate on behalf of clients, the firm has carved out a new niche of professionals in the commercial real estate industry. It has deliberately set itself apart from commercial brokers by offering clients three distinct differences that make it, in essence, the "anti-broker."

Cardinal employs **educated professionals** who can deliver a level of expertise that other brokers cannot do because they have no ties to specific companies or broker networks. The principals have years of institutional real estate experience and are part of a team of skilled consultants—i.e., lawyers, architects, project managers, and engineers.

Cardinal has designed **four proprietary processes** and numerous knowledge products for buying, selling, leasing, or acquiring/disposing of public assets. Each process outlines the best path to meeting your goals, with a detailed analysis of your specific needs, a customized strategy, extensive due diligence, and marketplace analysis.

For sellers: The Comprehensive Asset Sale™
For buyers: The Real Estate Capital Investment Review™
For tenants: The Strategic Tenant Advocate™
For public assets: The Public Asset Maximization Process™

Cardinal has set in place **accountability** at a level previously unheard of in the broker industry. With each client, Cardinal

determines and agrees upon a series of Key Performance
Indicators (KPIs) for measuring the success of your deal. After
the closing, Cardinal reviews the outcome and level of your satisfaction, then bases its compensation on the extent to which it
achieved your goals.

There is a better way to broker.

For more information, contact:

John Culbertson
Cardinal Real Estate Partners, LLC
200 South Tryon Street, Suite 1450 • Charlotte, NC 28202
Tel: 704-953-5500
jculbertson@cardinal-partners.com

55920031R00072

Made in the USA
Columbia, SC
19 April 2019